BURT FRANKLIN: RESEARCH & SOURCE WORKS SERIES 634
American Classics in History and Social Science 167

THE

PHILOSOPHICAL RADICALS

OF

1832

THE

PHILOSOPHICAL RADICALS

OF

1832

COMPRISING

THE LIFE OF SIR WILLIAM MOLESWORTH

AND SOME

INCIDENTS CONNECTED WITH THE REFORM

MOVEMENT FROM 1832 TO 1842

by

HARRIET GROTE

BURT FRANKLIN
New York   N. Y.

923.242

M717g

235 East 44th St., New York, N.Y. 10017
Originally Published: 1866
Reprinted: 1970
Printed in the U.S.A.

S.B.N.: 8337-14617
Library of Congress Card Catalog No.: 72-133543
Burt Franklin: Research and Source Works Series 634
American Classics in History and Social Science 167

Reprinted from the original edition in the University of California
Library.

INTRODUCTION.

THIS memoir has been composed partly with a view to enable a younger generation to understand the events of the period to which the narrative relates. Having been in a position to observe the working of the political forces during that singularly interesting passage—the passing of the Reform Bill—I felt myself moved to write some account of the personal agency exercised by certain individuals in directing the course of public opinion.

It is not a history of the Reformed Parliament: I wish it were; for so vigorous and healthy an effort to amend our political machinery would form a worthy subject for any pen. My sketch is, for the most part, a personal one; yet whilst it will do justice to the merits of a departed statesman, it may also assist future students of English domestic history to acquire a more complete view of the character of a memorable movement, from its energetic commencement in 1832, to its decline in 1842.

The elections which took place at the end of 1832 called into the political arena a considerable number of new men, amongst whom many were qualified by their intelligence and capacity to play an important part in the business of legislation.

Of these, two figures may, by persons of mature age at least, be recalled to memory, as forming perhaps the most prominent members of the section known as the " Philosophical Radicals." The one was Mr. George Grote, member for the City of London; the other was Sir William Molesworth, who represented his native county of Cornwall.

The first was then approaching the meridian of life, having reached his thirty-eighth year. He had been trained to political studies in the severe school of Bentham and Mill and other profound thinkers, and had also possessed the advantage of personal intimacy with David Ricardo, whilst cultivating the (at that time nascent) science of Political Economy.

The second, yet in the flower of youth, and des-tined soon to become the disciple of his elder col-league, was but slightly indebted to others for the instruction he had acquired. He had laid up, chiefly by private study, no inconsiderable store of learning and scientific knowledge, but, in regard to mental philosophy and political doctrine, he might be said to bring into public life as it were a virgin intellect.

It is to these two figures that the following pages are principally devoted. The character and history of Sir William Molesworth will be found portrayed with a full pencil—his untimely disappearance from amongst us admitting of this comparatively free treatment.

Of the other subject of this fragmentary memoir, so much as is personal has been advisedly touched with a more sober tone of colour, in harmony with the reverence due to one still living, and to the relation in which the writer has the honour and happiness to stand towards him.

March, 1866.

CONTENTS.

CHAPTER I.

ON the meeting of the first Reform Parliament, in February, 1833, Mr. Grote took his seat as Member for the City of London, having (I may be allowed to add) come in at the head of the poll. As we had no residence in London, except our house in Thread-needle-street, adjoining the banking house, we took lodgings at Mr. Oakley's, the grocer's, corner of Parliament-street and Bridge-street, in order to be nearer to the scene of business on the commence-ment of so very interesting and auspicious an era in political affairs. Some weeks elapsed, when one evening Mr. Grote said to me, "H. there is a young man who sometimes talks to me on our side of the House, of whom I have formed rather a good opinion; he is a Cornish baronet, of the name of Sir William Molesworth, and sits for his native county. I should like to bring him here, and intro-duce him to you." Shortly afterwards Mr. Grote accordingly brought Sir William home to tea with us, and he made a very favourable impression on us both. After this introduction, as he knew scarcely anybody else except the Buller family (also Cornish by race), he naturally frequented our lodgings when-

B

ever his public duties allowed of it. In the month
of May, 1833, he offered himself to accompany us
on a little rural tour into the county of Surrey and
into Hampshire during the Whitsuntide recess.
Mrs. Austin had engaged herself to be of the party.
Sir William and Mr. Grote rode on horseback, and
Mrs. Austin went with me in my phaeton, which I
drove myself. Molesworth was just then three-and-
twenty;* he had a pleasant countenance, expressive
blue eyes, florid complexion, and light brown hair;
a slim and neatly made figure, about five feet ten in
height, with small well-shaped hands and feet. He
rode well; and his manners were, when he took the
trouble, those of a man accustomed to good company
and assiduous to please. This tour naturally threw
us into relations of familiar intimacy, which were
sustained by frequent visits to us afterwards at our
residence near London; Molesworth often staying
the Saturday and Sunday at Dulwich Wood.

During the Parliamentary sessions of 1834, '35, '36,
Molesworth was a regular *habitué* of our society.
He contracted an earnest admiration and esteem for
Mr. Grote, to whom he looked up as a disciple might
to a master, whilst in myself he found an indulgent
friend and monitress. I liked and esteemed his noble,
frank, and chivalrous character, and took pleasure
in affording him the privilege of unreserved and con-
fidential intercourse. His political character, during
the first years of our intimate communion, was
that of a determined and unflinching Reformer. It
appeared by his own statement, that he had not
intended to enter into political life so soon as he
actually did.† He was residing in Italy in 1830-'31,
where he blended intellectual pursuits and studies
with a love of pleasure in a somewhat remarkable

---

* His twenty-third birth-day occurred during this excursion.
† See Sir William's own statement made to me in 1840, p. 52.

degree. A near relative of mine, who formed one of a small knot of intimate friends around Sir William Molesworth at this period, has more than once related to me (not without remarking upon the singularity of the fact), that although Molesworth willingly joined in the frolics, the fun, the follies, and I may add, the vices, of his light-hearted companions, he never failed to consecrate the whole of his morning to serious study. Indeed he was in 1831 actually employed in acquiring more than one of the Oriental languages, with a view to undertaking more extensive travels in Turkey and Asia. The science which, however, most fascinated and interested him, was that of Pure Mathematics, of which he had, I have reason to believe, made himself a complete master: so much so, that, many years subsequent, he told me that the study had lost its interest in some sort for him, since he now comprehended the limits of its exercise, and that the pursuit therefore had ceased to stimulate his intellectual curiosity. Molesworth was indeed, at this time, surprisingly accomplished for his age. Deeply imbued with a love of letters and of intellectual science in general, he had acquired more knowledge in the field of literature, both ancient and modern, than is commonly possessed by young men in his position. It happened that, partly from the circumstances of his education, partly from the native strength of his understanding, he had formed his political opinions in a sense diametrically opposite to those of his contemporary acquaintances and the gentry of his county. He had studied theology, and repudiated the Christian mysteries, refused to attend church, and laughed at those who did. He disliked aristocratic institutions, detested ecclesiastical government, felt earnestly the injustice and wrongs under which the bulk of the English people suffered, and longed to assist in bringing about a healthier and more just scheme of domestic administration.

Entertaining these opinions, he could not resist the call which was made upon him by certain Reformers in his native county, to come back to England and to put himself at the head of the movement which was stirring England to its centre, and which vibrated to her remotest provinces. He was returned for the county without difficulty, although personally little known and that little not favourably; but as being a large landowner, and coming of an ancient Cornish family, he fulfilled the conditions which, in 1832, were principally required in a candidate for a county representation.

I have already said that he knew scarcely any one, and, what is singular, he desired to know none, refusing all advances from other quarters, and confining his society almost entirely to the Bullers and ourselves. In the summer of 1833, he talked to me of the probability of his settling in life. Since he had come into Parliament, he said, it would be necessary to live in England, and, living in England, it would be desirable for him to marry. I said that I agreed in his views, and presently asked him whether he had anybody in his eye. He replied that he had; that, as a youth, he had contracted a feeling of preference for Miss Julia Carew, the daughter of a country gentleman of that name, who lived at a seat called "Antony," not far from Plymouth. To this house Molesworth had been in the habit of riding over, with his servant carrying his saddle-bags (about thirty miles), and spending a couple or three days at a time, prior to his journey to Italy, when he was indeed very young and susceptible.

To return: he said that Miss Julia Carew would be the object of his matrimonial aims. Accord- ingly, on returning into Cornwall, and during the recess, he renewed his visits to Antony, and strove to recommend himself to the lady. I am justified in the belief that the young lady was not indifferent to

his attentions, and Sir William's suit might probably
have been attended with success, but for the opposition raised against it by Miss Carew's family. This
opposition stung him to the quick, whilst it fanned
the flame of his attachment. When Parliament met
in 1834, he endeavoured to engage Mrs. C. Buller's
good offices in bringing about opportunities for meeting the young lady. I remember well seeing Molesworth talking to Miss Carew at one of Mrs. Buller's
parties, on which occasion his manner and the ani-
mation of his countenance lent a singular charm to
his whole appearance. He obtained permission to
visit at the house of the Countess of St. Germans
(half-sister to Miss Julia Carew), in Park-crescent,
Portland-place; and so far advanced in his hopes as
to obtain from the young lady the assurance that she
would leave the decision to her kinsman, Lord
Lyttelton. If that nobleman, to whom she referred
Sir William for his sanction, should give his consent
to their union, she would no longer withhold her
own. Accordingly, without a moment's loss of time, to
Hagley flew the impatient lover, as fast as four post-
horses could convey him. Lord Lyttelton received
him with polite *hauteur;* Molesworth addressed him
in very earnest language, beseeching him to terminate
his anxieties by a favourable reply. His lordship
said that he understood him to be both a Radical in
politics and an infidel in religion. Molesworth
rejoined that he did not see what that could have to
do with his conduct or character, upon which he
challenged scrutiny. Lord Lyttelton then dryly said
that he could never advise his niece to unite herself
with a man of such obnoxious opinions. A somewhat animated discussion ensued, but his lordship
was inflexible. Molesworth left the house, and returned to London, travelling all night. The first
thing he did after alighting at his own lodgings and
refreshing himself, was to jump into his tilbury and

drive down to Dulwich Wood, with a view to relate the history of the last twenty-four hours to his sympathizing friend, who had all along kept *au courant* of the whole affair; but it happened that I had gone up to London that morning to be present at a concert at the Opera House Concert-room in the Haymarket. Thither poor Sir William tracked me, and, paying his half-guinea at the door, soon found himself by my side, to my astonishment. As soon as the piece then singing was over, he whispered me, " Pray come out into the ante-room, I have much to tell you." When we got by ourselves he narrated what was given above, only with more detail. He was in a perfect fever, his eyes flashing fire and fury, his voice full of emotion; and when at length we parted, he exclaimed, using a vehement gesture with his arm, " I vow to pull down this haughty aristocracy of ours, or perish in the attempt!"

From this time, finding hope well nigh extinguished, and that Miss Carew feared to brave the displeasure of her kindred—I may add the world's opinion—he began to lose heart in regard to this pursuit, and flung himself into study and politics with additional zeal. He now passed most of his leisure time at our place near Dulwich, where he used to meet Roebuck, C. Buller, Warburton, Prescott, Charles Austin and his sister, and others, in whose company he always shone. I remember driving my phaeton to London one morning, with Molesworth by my side, C. Buller and Roebuck in the seat behind. During the whole six miles, these three vied with each other as to who should make the most outrageous Radical motions in the House, the two behind standing up and talking, *sans intermission*, all the way, to Molesworth and myself.

He retired to Pencarrow after the recess, and occupied himself for a space in county gaieties and in making his own house agreeable; but he was never well looked upon by the Cornish families, for the same reasons which had prompted Lord Lyttelton's rejection. It must be added that the terrible wound to his self-love, involving also the extinction of his hopes of a happy marriage, both soured and indisposed him to court the good opinion of the neighbouring gentlemen. At the Plymouth races and balls Sir William again met the lady of his heart, and not long afterwards received, through her brothers (who paid him a visit at Pencarrow of a week's duration,) a general and cordial invitation to Antony from Mr. Carew. He went, of course; was attentive, but did not make much progress, being somewhat embarrassed by the presence of an observant and stiff family circle. He met her again at Mr. and Mrs. C. Buller's, at Polvellan, and there received, through his hostess, an intimation that he might possibly succeed, on condition of his renouncing, or at any rate modifying, his sceptical opinions. As he was far too honourable to dissemble on this subject, even to gain so wished-for a prize, he retired with a wounded spirit from the vain pursuit in the autumn of 1834, writing me a long account of his summer's adventures in a letter, part of which I here subjoin.

"Pencarrow, October, 1834.

.   .   .   .   .   .

"I have not seen her for a month, and another will elapse ere I have the slightest probability of meeting her again. Indeed, what between the various alternations of hope, fear, and anxiety, I have been so annoyed and vexed that I am completely disgusted with myself and irritated at my folly. I would do anything, not dishonourable, to gain the lady. I have softened down my opinions to the verge of falsehood; but that barrier I will not pass.

"I have been living a great deal on the wide world and on horseback. Years have elapsed since I have led so reckless a life. In spite of it—in spite of the deepest potations—in spite of the severest fatigue—I never was so well in my life! Some time will elapse, I am afraid, ere your prognostic will be fulfilled that I shall not live long. Indeed, I have just commenced Plato, in the Greek, though I have not opened a Greek book for ten years; and intend to peruse Aristotle and him previous to my departure to the *land of shades.* I have not been idle, however, I have an article, *Deo* (John Mill) *volente,* for the Review, which is, I hope, prospering. John is in such spirits that he says he would make it succeed single-handed. Old Mill will write, consequently we shall be *respectable.* Wilson, I believe, rules the *Globe;* Charles Buller assists him, and has written some excessively good articles lately upon the Church and Dissenter questions. I have contributed some on secondary punishments, transportation, &c. Mrs. A. is in town. I received a letter some days ago from her, in which she asked certain questions, which I do not intend and which I hope you will not answer. (*Sic* in orig.) Ask Grote what interesting new German works he has got. I have been reading a life of Alex. the Great by Drohsen, with which I am much pleased; likewise a history of Greek Philosophy, by Ritter. Write soon, and believe me, dear Mrs. Grote,

" Yours, most sincerely obedient,

(Signed)   " William Molesworth."

CHAPTER II.

DURING the autumn of 1834 Sir William occupied himself much with his new duties as proprietor and manager of the *London and Westminster Review*, of which he now undertook the pecuniary responsibility, having for his London editor a young man whose talents were then dawning upon the world of intellect—Mr. John Stuart Mill. Sir William was himself composing more than one article for this periodical, and studying various subjects in preparation for the coming session. Part of a letter which I received from him in October, 1834, is here inserted, and will be read with interest.

"Pencarrow, October, 1834.

. . . . . .

"You are desirous of knowing something of our Review. Each account seems to be more favourable, and so heartily have all—*almost* all, I mean—of those similar in principles to ourselves, taken up the subject, that I am most sanguine of success. The prospectus will soon (I hope early next month) be issued, and I will take care you receive one. We shall be delighted if you approve of it, and if you should like to write, we will, I dare say, have much pleasure in inserting your article, provided you are not too violent. The first number will be out in January ; the list of articles and of the writers is such as to promise much. What between those who have promised to be regular and certain contributors, and those who are to be occasional ones, the prospect for the subsequent numbers is excellent. . . . . I believe I told you that, in order that the conductors may merely be answerable for the general principles advocated, not for the particular development of them and in order to attach a certain degree of responsibility to each writer, some signature is to be affixed to each article. We intend, not merely to keep to politics, but to attempt to develop the philosophy of society—of the human mind—of imaginative literature and ethics—at least so the prospectus states. . . . . Give my best regards to Grote, and entreat him to write the article on Swiss Politics : it will be most interesting.

"Believe me ever yours,

"Most sincerely obedient,

(Signed) "WM. MOLESWORTH."

A new Parliament was elected in the winter of 1834—'35—a most exciting struggle it was, seeing that the Tory party played their strongest, having possession of the Government. I append, as a sample of the proceedings of the period, a letter written to a friend (also engaged in a contest for a seat in Parliament) about the election for the City of London, always among the earliest at a general election. Sir William took the warmest interest in Mr. Grote's success, looking to him as his lawful leader in politics, and adjusting his own line of conduct by that of his older friend.*

* I may cite an instance. On one occasion, during the session of, I think, 1836, the repeal of the malt-tax being hotly debated, Molesworth voted for keeping up the tax—contrary to the views of most of the Radical members. One of these, discovering soon after that the vote he himself had given was an injudicious vote, asked Sir William " how it was that he had been able to see so clearly what was the wise course ?" " Well, but I did not see it," replied Sir William. " Did you not ? Why, then, did you vote as you did?" " Because I saw Grote going out, and I followed him —because I was afraid to vote otherwise than he did ; but I own to you that I did so with fear and trembling."

The letter will furnish an idea of the active and zealous efforts made by the Liberals, or, as they were then willing to be termed, the Radicals, of the City of London.

"Monday, 29th December, 1834.

" MY DEAR MRS. GASKELL,

"One line is all I have time or power to write, but such a piece of luck as I have to tell *must* be sent to you for participation. Our City 'Rads' have been working most assiduously, and striving to obtain a fourth man, *in case*, and *only* in case, the Tories called forth Mr. Ward. You cannot conceive a finer set of hearty, yet wise and judicious men, than we boast among our middle class in London ! Mr. Grote is daily, and almost hourly, in communication with them, and aiding, by his personal exertions, the great object of giving a signal example to the country at our coming election. Well, my dear friend, after many anxious conferences, after trying the temper of the Tories, and finding Ward was actually going to provoke a contest (which, observe, WE wished to avoid, for fear of mischief), we actually have prevailed on no less a personage than *the Governor of the Bank of England* to start as our fourth Reformer ! ! !

" I assure you I think it is the proudest day of my husband's life. He never had so great a consciousness of being useful, even though we have had our trials and *eke* our triumphs, and he is in better spirits than I ever saw him ; and this, after being, all last week, so agitated and careworn that I am sure you would have been quite pained to see him : so apprehensive was he about getting a good fourth man, and if *not* ' a good one,' he feared *defeat*.

" Mr. Pattison, the new candidate, is one of the oldest and most intimate friends of Mr. Grote's family, and he has become liberalized by communion with him, as well as by Grote's writings and speeches in Parliament. He had no wish, nay, even a repugnance, to enter public life, (he is about forty-five years of age I think,) but, pressed by the citizens in the first place, he was won finally by Grote's earnest entreaty to step forward and fight by his side, and he could not refuse to do so, feeling a confidence that Grote would support him and set him a wise lead. He is Reformer enough to satisfy our ' movement,' and his station and personal character command the votes and confidence of the *timid rich* voters ; so that it is impossible to over-estimate the importance to Reformers of this step on his part. We imagine the Tories will be planet-struck at the firing of this our *great gun !*

" We are all agitation and fervour in London. I only pray you may be doing half as well in your parts. Excuse my conjugal vanity, but you can't think how I run over with emotion when I reflect that Grote has, by courageously standing in the van, encouraged less bold and wise patriots to step out of the crowd, and has thus, in his person, redeemed the representation of his city, the first in the empire, by attracting to it men of station and honour, instead of the despicable corporation nominees of ancient times. You see how he has dragged on his colleague Crawford, who now goes the full length with him. The fact is Grote leaves them no choice but to keep pace with him in public opinion. We shall have a ' Four Reformers' Consolidated Committee,' and canvass accordingly, no individual asking for himself. Ours will be among the earliest elections, and, I trust, ' a light to lighten the Gentiles.' Hurrah ! God bless you, my dear Mrs. G., I embrace you cordially as a faithful sympathizer in the sentiments of

" Yours affectionately,

(Signed) " H. Grote."

For two years or more Molesworth had frequented the society of Mr. Mill (the elder), deriving much instruction from communion with that gentleman's sagacious and powerful mind. He continued to gain on the esteem and friendship of Mr. Grote and myself, proving himself indeed a well-informed, zealous, and effective partizan of political progress. At Mrs. C. Buller's house (who had now taken a house next door to Jeremy Bentham's in Queen-square, Westminster) Sir William was a frequent guest, and habitually found there her niece, Miss Jane Strachey, a very pretty young person, of good understanding, and by no means devoid of talent. After a certain time the young baronet found himself becoming strongly attracted towards this lady, and about the end of June he made her an offer of his hand :* a step which, it may be observed, produced evident satisfaction in the mind of the aunt. Nevertheless *this* suit was also destined to be unprosperous; for the mother (a widow of Mr. Edward Strachey, a brother of Sir Henry Strachey, Bart.—*father* there was no longer,) demurred to the proposal on the ground of Sir William's undisguised scepticism. This lady was a rigorous Calvinist, who regarded with horror and aversion the notion of her daughter marrying a man who, as it was said, questioned the divinity of Jesus Christ. After many *pourparlers,* and some rather acrimonious correspondence, Sir William retired from the position of an aspirant; the young lady being under age, and the mother inexorable. His regard and affection for Miss Strachey appear to have been very sincere; and many passages in his letters to me about that period reflect much credit on his behaviour throughout this, to him, painful affair. That Miss Strachey, if left to herself, would have accepted him I had reason to believe probable, as also that Mrs. Buller would have been well pleased to number him amongst her relations.

I insert here portions of a letter received from Sir William in the autumn of 1835. They show with how much earnest devotion to serious studies he at this time employed his leisure. His mind had been disturbed by the love affair above mentioned, and he seemed desirous of banishing the recollection of it by plunging into books and work. After giving

---

* Sir William was, with Mr. Grote and myself, a guest at the house of our friend James Mill, during a Saturday and Sunday in June, 1835. We all strolled in the meadows under Norbury Park after dinner, and, during the walk, Molesworth disclosed to me his intention of proposing to Miss Strachey. He obviously felt deeply anxious as to his chance of success, but was far from anticipating the resistance which his suit was destined to encounter.

me a list of the articles in hand for the *London and Westminster Review*, he goes on to say—

"You ask what I am about? Studying Epicurus, reading everything I can find in innumerable authors with regard to him. Object I have in view is, the history of philosophy during the time of Thomas Hobbes. Gassendus, who was an intimate friend of Hobbes, and from whom, I believe, the latter derived much, was an Epicurean philosopher, and has written a large folio volume upon the subject, which I am in the act of perusing. Now I want to know what in reality were the opinions of Epicurus. . . . . . . I intend, as the immediate result of my labours, some time or another to write two articles: one on the Metaphysics of Epicurus, the other on the Ethics. The first one I think I have nearly mastered, and you may expect to see it some six or nine months hence in ' *The London.*' The Ethics will be more troublesome. However I shall set to soon. . . . . . . *A propos de bottes*—did you see my speech against the Lords and conciliation? The accursed reporters said my speech was so violent that they could not report it, and altered it most considerably."

Molesworth came to town at Christmas, 1835-6, and I have an entry in my note-book of his dining with us on January 3rd, 1836, at Dulwich Wood. The recent change of administration and the advent of Sir Robert Peel caused a good deal of excitement among political circles, whilst the momentous measures in respect of domestic legislation, passed in 1835, viz., the Poor Law Act and the Municipal Corporations Bill, occasioned no small gratulation among the members of the Radical camp.

The fourth number of the *London Review* came forth in January, 1836, and well sustained its reputation, Mr. James Mill and his son, Mr. Charles Buller, Mr. Peacock, and other able writers furnishing a paper each. Indeed it is worthy of note here that the elder Mill was at this time a dying man, yet felt it a pleasure to assist Sir William with his latest powers. The first number of this periodical, after it took the title of the *London and Westminster Review*, appeared in April of this year, and contained an article the fame of which has survived to the present day, viz., A View of the Political Condition of France," by M. Alexis de Tocqueville. There was likewise in this number a capital history of Orange lodges from the pen of Sir William himself. On this subject, too, he made a spirited and effective speech or two in the House of Commons.*

* In the early part of the summer of 1836, Sir William had a severe attack of illness, the nature of which was erysipelas in the region of the brain. In fact, the premonitory symptoms were discerned by myself, late on one afternoon, at our rooms at Fendall's Hotel, in Westminster—Sir William having called on me there. I persuaded him to go home to his lodgings, close by, and to send for his doctor at once. He did so, and was fortunately able to get through the attack without worse consequences than a certain amount of debility, caused by the treatment adopted. It will be seen, later, how this unlucky illness affected his arrangements for passing the months of September and October.

CHAPTER III.

SIR W. MOLESWORTH DETERMINES ON RELINQUISHING HIS
SEAT FOR THE COUNTY, BUT INTENDS TRYING SOME OTHER
CONSTITUENCY.

DURING the Session of 1836, which ended by the
Whigs driving Sir Robert Peel from the Government,
Sir William had, as I have already stated, sustained
his reputation, and justified the expectations of his
friends, by the exhibition of growing capacity and
added knowledge, as well as by the perfect consistency
and courage of his political course. But neither he
nor Mr. Grote had taken any lively interest in pro-
moting the return to power of the Whig party, having
found, by the experience of four years of their reign,
how much less of good was to be expected from
them than was at first hoped for by their Radical
allies. After their reinstatement, in fact, Sir William
cherished a certain longing for the resumption of a
studious and leisurely existence; towards which ten-
dency his doubts about retaining his seat for East
Cornwall in some measure contributed. He used to
talk in this strain with me, not unfrequently, and
urged, in support of his wishes to quit Parliament,
that he should be more useful and influential by
concentrating his talents and energies upon the
London Review, now confessedly the ablest periodical,
on the Liberal side, going. Although I could not but
comprehend the feeling which would lead a man of
Molesworth's fortune and independent habits of

thought to withdraw from politics, and enjoy his comfortable seat in Cornwall, surrounded by books, and free from the conflict of hostile opinions, I could not bear the idea of his quitting the small band of " Philosophical Radicals " (as we were termed) so early in the course of the Reform movement. Nevertheless we left England at the close of the Session, without seeing our way to Molesworth's future with any certainty; the only thing we seemed to *know* being that his re-election for East Cornwall was extremely doubtful. Mr. Grote and I went in August on a tour in France, through Normandy, returning by the banks of the Loire, and during this journey I wrote a letter to Sir William, pressing upon him the duty of continuing to assist us in Parliament, notwithstanding his growing disinclination to its labours, and suggesting that he should look out for another seat, &c. &c. I pause a moment here to mention an affair unconnected with politics, in which Sir William was anxiously interested.

The sentiments which he had early entertained towards Miss Carew revived in 1836, to so strong a degree that Sir William again endeavoured to overcome her scruples, and to induce her to accept his homage. During the London season of this year he even made certain concessions, on the score of his opinions, in the view of gaining her favour and disarming the objections of her uncle. These sacrifices were attended with much pain to his conscience, but they did not bring about the effect aimed at. Writing to me in August, he uses these expressions:—

" I hope Mrs. Buller has not the slightest idea of what I was about before I left London. . . . . Now that I can coolly reflect, I think the whole of that business must now be over, and I am glad to have bound myself so solemnly to avoid her presence. . . . . The manner of her uncle to me will remain ever in my memory, with a feeling of deep and lasting re- venge. . . . . May we meet some day on even terms, and he

C

shall know that one who once crouched to him in humility can and will repay contempt with bitter and biting scorn. . ."

Sir William had felt the necessity of a little change and recreation, and he accordingly set forth, in July, on a tour in Germany,* accompanied by his mother and his surviving sister (the eldest having died a few months before this), taking up Mr. Francis Molesworth at Frankfort. This young man had been for some years under the care and tuition of a Dr. Bekker, A.M., at Offenbach; Sir William deeming a German education preferable to an English one for his brother: moreover Sir William had himself been placed with Dr. Bekker for a time, after leaving Edinburgh.

A letter, which I had written in August to Sir William, found him at Prague, it would seem, on the 4th Sept. 1836, and he replied on the same day. I give here the greater portion of his letter, which reached me on 14th Sept., at Paris.

"Prague, September 4, 1836.

"My dear Mrs. Grote,

"Many thanks for your kind letter, which I received to-day along with that of Grote, to which I shall first reply. I wrote, about a fortnight before I left England, to my agents, Mr. Leach and Mr. Woollcombe, with regard to my prospects for Cornwall in the event of a dissolution. Both of them are intimately acquainted with the state of affairs there. I told them my apprehensions—my unwillingness to incur any con-

---

* He wrote me a letter of adieu, just before leaving England (dated July, 1836), of which the following are extracts:—" My brother and I are going to read Greek together on the outside of the carriage, and we have got a brace of Thucydides in order to study history. . . . . John Mill was here this morning, and we settled certain preliminaries for next year's campaign. I told him of no less than five motions which I intend to originate, and the speeches for which I trust will be finished ere I again see you—and in thus saying, deep is my grief when I contemplate the long period of separation, and in bidding adieu for some months to you, who have truly been to me since I first knew you my kindest and sincerest friend. . . . . Pray write to me soon; if you will direct to me, at Frankfurt, A.M., Koch the banker will forward it to me.

" W. Molesworth."

siderable expense ; at the same time I said that I had not the slightest objection to expend a thousand pounds. Their answer, on mature consideration, was, that I should fight with a strong probability of defeat, on account of the present defection of the Whigs ; that I was certain of defeat whenever a decided separation between Whigs and Radicals took place ; and, lastly, I should incur a very considerable expense, which it was absurd to think of limiting to a thousand pounds. Their advice was, that it would be most consistent with my honour and principles to immediately state my intention of not standing again for Cornwall. . . . .

"Before I received the letters of Mr. Leach and Mr. Woollcombe, I was far from thinking of the step which they proposed, though I had been previously informed by the leader of the Whigs that he would not support me, and my colleague advised me not to register, as I should find the Whigs against me.

"Upon the cool and deliberate advice of my agents, I determined to act. Unfortunately, I was very ill, and my places were taken for the Continent. Buller came to my rooms. I wrote my address in haste, and left it with him to correct, and to ask the opinions of my friends. He wrote to me to say they approved of my giving up Cornwall (which is likewise Grote's opinion under the circumstances of the case), and sent me a corrected copy of my address, which, long ere this, must have been printed.

"I am much obliged to him for the trouble which he has taken. . . . . I was, in truth, excessively glad to find any one to aid me. Now, with regard to the rest of your letter, I think you are wrong in accusing me of an absolute wish to shrink from the combat; on the contrary, I stated my anxious hope of being of service to the cause through the *London** ; and as long as *that Review* is carried on with energy, you cannot accuse me of deserting the party. I did certainly indulge in a feeling of pleasure at the idea of being once again free from the trammels of Parliament, and sought out reasons for justifying this feeling in your eyes ; but, in truth, I will do exactly as you like, for you are the only person who is invariably kind to me whenever I commit follies or errors, and whose reproofs even sound to me more pleasing than the praises of others. I will come into Parliament again, if you wish it, and if I can get a constituency that will take me with a clear declaration of my opinions. I am glad that I am free

* The *Review*.

from Cornwall, for I was in a most painful situation there, with hardly a gentleman to support me.

" With regard to Westminster, I don't care at all for Ward, if the Westminster men are such as I take them to be ; and I have not the slightest hesitation or scruple with regard to him (Ward). I am much obliged to Place for his offer to organize Westminster for me. I will write to him upon the subject. I wish you would write to him likewise. You say, however, you do not recommend me to stand for Westminster, but that I ' must use my own discretion.' Now, ' my discretion' would be this : if well-informed persons think there would be a good chance of my succeeding, I would stand in opposition to the devil, more especially if he had any Whig inclinations, and will come to England as soon as it would be necessary. Pray *consider* for me, and write to me, *post restante*, Berlin. Do not be offended at my asking you to assist me so much; and remember that the conclusion of your letter contained a command not to desert you.

" I am much obliged to you (and if I were not I should be a most ungrateful scoundrel) for your having performed my request with regard to Miss Strachey, though I am grieved at your denying my position ' that she never cared for me ;' this position I am determined to believe, so pray don't contradict it again, otherwise I should have to reproach myself with doing what I trust I have never done, and never will do, viz., playing with a young woman's affections. I don't feel *so* clear in my conscience as not to cling earnestly to the belief I have stated. I do not much approve of your likening me to Victor Alfieri, for though there be but little really to esteem in him, nevertheless there is a feeling of romance about him which is apt to catch a woman's fancy ; and though I should not wish to be thought ill of by her, I wish never to be present to her mind : more especially if any feelings of liking ever did exist, and romance keeps that accursed sentiment alive which has made such a fool of me, I hope for the last time. You do not understand that it is the Corn-laws and my votes on agricultural questions which affect my seat, and which afford a plea for deserting me : my staunchest supporters are in the habit of saying that I should be an excellent member for a city, but that I have not sufficient regard for the agricultural interest. You would not have wished me to compromise those questions, nor could I have done it with my *Review ;* indeed, I knew it (the *Review*) would lose me my seat, and it was the first pretext against me. I was called upon to deny certain opinions in one of John's political articles. I refused to do so, and the leader of the Whigs, Sir Colman Rashleigh, immediately wrote to me that he would not support me.

" I am afraid that the egotism which pervaded the last letter will be found in this ; for it entirely concerns ' what will suit W. M.'s particular views and objects.' I am afraid that I *am* terribly egotistical, and am becoming more and more so. I am horribly selfish—not that I care what becomes of me, but everything turns upon ' I ;' and if it were not for you disturbing every now and then the reveries upon ' I,' I should be *all* '*I.*'

" Would you like to know what is going on here ? The cholera, they say, is raging fearfully. Mary says we are a family who laugh at death, and have no fears, thanks to me ; so we do not mind it. Great care is taken to conceal the ravages, and the people are buried during the night. The ceremonies for the coronation commenced on the first (Sept.) with the solemn entry of the emperor ; a pretty sight, but nothing remarkable. [Here follows a description of Prague, the opera, music, &c.] To-morrow I am to be presented to the emperor. . . . . Thus we intend to see all the sights, and then depart for Dresden. My youngest brother, whom you saw at Offenbach, is with me. He is an excessively fine boy, and speaks German like a German. He will fill my shoes well, for I feel my career will be a short one, and my second brother's not much longer. I like the system I have pursued in educating Francis abroad ; it gives him an independent feeling and self-reliance, which is most valuable. Prescott is with you, I suppose. Pray give my best regards to him. There are few persons for whom I have a sincerer esteem than for him. With best regards to Grote, and thanks for his letter, which I have answered in writing to you, believe me, my dear Mrs. Grote,

" Yours most truly and sincerely,

(Signed) " WILLIAM MOLESWORTH."

The following letter serves to throw light upon Sir William Molesworth's political *status* at this period :—

Extract of Letter from Jos. Parkes to Mrs. Grote.

" With respect to Molesworth—and no one can more heartily admire and honour him than I do—I have long said that he is the only *leading* public mind in the House of Commons, thrown up by the Reform Bill : that is to say, the only *propelling* mind there who did not participate in the glorious pull *we* had for the modicum of Parliamentary Reform gained in 1832. Though not wholly concurring in Molesworth's Cornish ' *deploy,*' don't think I am such a fool as not to see the *immense shove* he has given, and is giving the Ballot, and the bolder front and ground he is ' general-ing' the Reformers of the empire to take in the approaching contest with the aristocracy ; but Molesworth is only *one*. He has much apprenticeship yet to serve, and much temptation yet to resist. That experience will make him a much *more* powerful public man, and that his principles will protect him against political seductions, I do not doubt. . . . .

" I know all about Molesworth's ' Cornish hug' of the Whigs from himself months since : from the Cornish and Devon corporate deputies up here about ' charities,' and from Molesworth's agent, &c."

I felt it a duty to sound some of the influential London Reformers about Westminster for Molesworth. Parkes gave it as his opinion that Ward must not be opposed, though he regarded Ward as certain to pass into office ere long; yet he had a sort of Radical reputation, and it would be impolitic to obstruct his election by starting another Radical. Mr. John Travers, who whilst he lived exercised considerable power over the metropolitan electors, wrote to me thus :—

Extract of Letter from the late John Travers, of Swithin's-lane.

" Of Sir William Molesworth I think there can hardly be two opinions that he would suit such a constituency as West-minster *well.* I should be delighted to see him there ; but, unless Evans retires, may it not be wanted for Mr. Hume ?"

Francis Place, the tailor, of Charing Cross, deemed it best for Sir William to keep his eye upon Maryle-bone (which borough he considered it probable would readily elect him) until the Westminster seat should seem more certainly open to his candidature than just then it could fairly be said to be.

Before Sir William returned to England, we had been hurried home by the alarming illness of Mr. Prescott, senior partner of the banking-house of which Mr. Grote was a member; and it was after our entering upon the occupation of our new residence (in Eccleston Street, Belgrave Square,) that I received a letter from Molesworth, dated Berlin, October 15, 1836. Extracts from this letter will be given in the next chapter.

CHAPTER IV.

1836. THE RADICAL PARTY ON THE DECLINE IN THE HOUSE
OF COMMONS.—CORRESPONDENCE ON POLITICAL AFFAIRS.

Sir William Molesworth to Mrs. Grote.

" October 15th, 1836.

" I SHALL probably have the pleasure of seeing you at the end
of this month (October), as I intend to leave this place for
Hamburgh on the 20th, on my road to England. I am, as
you may suppose, well pleased with the success of my address.
. . . . From the extracts in the papers sent by my friends
my conduct seems to have created a deep sensation ; and, if
report speaks true, Leeds and Bath both intend to offer me a
seat. I wrote to Place and Roebuck about Westminster.
Thompson* has an intention to stand for that place, and I
could not think of interfering with *him*. Perhaps, however,
two seats will be required, in which case I should prefer taking
my chance for Westminster, to being certain of a seat else-
where. I received a communication, in which it was stated
that Marylebone was anxious to have me. That, if I would
assent, a requisition would be got up, signed by three thousand
electors, who would bring me in free of expense. I
should like very well, if I *can't* get Westminster, to come in
for Marylebone, and I should relish defeating Henry Bulwer,
for his Whigism.

" You may suppose I am somewhat flattered by these com-
plimentary intentions, which will leave me but little chance of
that retired and philosophic life after which I longed, but the
impropriety of which you so clearly demonstrated. . . .

" The Whigs, I presume, now abuse me like a pickpocket.
They have not done with me, and they may be assured that
no love is lost between us. They would have been delighted
to have seen me defeated in Cornwall, and are furious at *my*
turning upon *them first*. I intend to do them more harm yet;
and, on the first opportunity, to tear to pieces that accursed

* Perronet Thompson.

cry of 'Union amongst Reformers!' by which they have disgraced the Radicals into the dishonoured followers of their debasing policy. . . . . .

"I presume you will see such of our friends as are in town, and I shall expect to learn from you a succinct account of the state of things in general. Pray see Place.

"I received a letter from Mrs. Buller a few days ago. She wrote from Manheim. She talks of Charles taking office under the Whigs—foolish woman! They will never give him anything; and if they would, he would only damage himself for the sake of that which can only be of the most temporary duration. . . .

"I wrote thus far a week ago, when I took it into my head to commence a Political Article for the next *London;* having finished all I intend to write of that at the present, I return to my letter to you. Pray use your influence over our friends, not again to attempt to raise the cry of 'Union amongst Reformers!'—so far from its producing 'union,' it will produce 'disunion'—as destroying all unity of purpose. Ballot, Triennial Parliaments, Extension of the Suffrage, and Reform of the House of Lords, are the only means by which the quiet progress of Reform can be secured. . . The cry of 'Union among Reformers!' can never be again raised with success. The people are indifferent to the Whigs, whilst the Radicals in the House, by their timidity, are losing *their* hold over the nation. By acting boldly, without reference to the existence or non-existence of the ministers, they will regain their influence, and rally round them a party which will be irresistible. . . Pray stir them up! See Rintoul. I read one of his articles, in which he talked of the Tories being in before Easter—most probably, and no harm either. Consider—the Whigs wont take the only means of doing anything, the Tories wont do anything. What is gained or lost by the one or the other in power? The prejudice of 'Union' must be attacked. . . When we meet, however, I expect to hear the feelings of our leaders. We ought to assemble to see if we can devise any line of policy, or are we to continue aimless and purposeless, doing nothing? I wish I were ten years older, and a ready and fluent orator. However, if they wont act, one must wish them adieu. . . I will dine with you on Sunday, the 30th. Ask some Rads. to meet me—honest men and true.

"Yours sincerely,

(Signed) "WILLIAM MOLESWORTH."

Thomas Falconer to H. Grote.

"Gray's Inn, 31st December, 1836.

"Dear Mrs. Grote,

"I am greatly obliged to you for the loan of the articles upon the Ballot, that appeared in the *Morning Chronicle*. I will return them at the earliest moment, but as I propose to copy a considerable part of them, I hope you will permit me to keep the book a few days. Miss Hale, by an accident, personally delivered the treasure to me—for which good act I am indebted. In return, I have promised to present the third number of *The London,* but I have not at present any but my own copy, and I believe that Macrone has not got copies. I will obtain a copy and send it. Parkes has written to me a most plaintive tale, and threatens the occurrence of terrible political disasters to Liberals. The ship must be in a bad state when he puts out signs of distress. He thinks Molesworth is to blame. Molesworth is not the aggressor. The Whigs threw the first stone, and endeavoured to exclude him from Parliament. He therefore insists upon the only measure which can in future prevent the success of such an attempt. He took two years' faithful apprenticeship to the Whigs, performed his servitude well—ready to continue —but time being considered 'up,' and being ill-treated by his masters, he 'opened shop' upon his own account. But, seriously, it appears to me to be exceedingly unjust to attack Molesworth for what he has done. He has had no choice; nor have the Radicals any choice. He and they must submit to be extinguished, or take a bolder lead than they have done. They have demonstrated to the Whigs that imperfect and very moderate political measures cannot be carried. The farce has continued long enough, and may now require better measures than have been offered for their acceptance.

"Parkes says that the constituencies are corrupt, and that we miscalculate our strength. If public opinion is against us, there ought not to be a Liberal ministry. But this is not the only reply. Is the honest portion of sincere and zealous Reformers to be disgusted, and to be deprived of the greatest incentive to exertion, by seeing their leaders, and those whom they are willing to trust, inactive, and silently following in the train of the Whigs at the moment when they expect from them the sincere and unmodified assertion of their principles? There is no wish to *turn out* the Whigs, but if they fall to pieces from want of union, or vigour of purpose, there is no reason why we should be covered with the rubbish.

> "Very sincerely yours,
>
> (Signed) "THOMAS FALCONER."

A letter addressed to myself (in 1836) by Mr. Warburton, M.P., will be read with interest here in connexion with Sir William's affairs. Mr. Warburton had been aware of Sir William's growing disinclination to continue in public life, and of the endeavours I had used to counteract it. The following extract relates to a letter of Sir William to myself:—

> "What you say about Molesworth, or rather what he says about himself, is so far satisfactory that he has not deserted politics, though there is an absurd morbid feeling about him, as being for this world for but a short period, and speaking of his brother as a 'promising successor.' What is this language in the mouth of a young fellow in the flower of youth? He must have been courting and disappointed in love, or he would never talk after this fashion. . . ."

That there was more foundation for this conjecture than Mr. Warburton knew of, has been shown already. Between the vexation arising from disappointment in love, and displeasure at the untoward course of Liberal politics, Sir William's mind became tinctured with a bitterness which prompted him to write in a tone such as I deemed it necessary to reprove him gently for employing. In reply, he wrote thus, in December, 1836:—

> "I see the *Spectator* and *Constitutional* are going very straight. You are one of the 'valued correspondents' of the former. I am sure I recognised you in the pother about the *Globe*. But what do you mean by saying that I am the only *respectable* Radical who was attacking ministers? I am not one of the respectables.
>
> "I was much pleased with your last letter. I should be a

brute indeed if I could willingly do anything to grieve you, after your much kindness to me. It is true what you say about public life destroying a man for the kindlier relations of social life. I told you this would be the case with me. I hesitated some time on the threshold. I am now embarked and hesitate no longer; no social feelings, nor friendships, nor anything else, shall stand in the way of my pushing my principles. . . . You have compared me to Victor Alfieri. I think there *is* some justice in the comparison. . . . I intend to prosecute a Newcastle paper for saying I am a ' wretch without a God;' that is, if the rascal in question does not comply with the humiliating terms I have prescribed to him. . . . I feel it is a duty I owe to society to prevent people falling foul of one's religious opinions.

" Leeds wont do. Too many Whigs there. I will play the devil there however; but probably will come to Westminster.

" Yours affectionately,

(Signed) " WILLIAM MOLESWORTH."

I find in my " Notes " of this period the following entry:—

" The upshot of the last six months is neither more nor less than the total extinction of the Parliamentary Radical party. They are absorbed into that of the Whigs. . . . . Mr. Grote and about five others find themselves left to sustain the Radical opinions of the House of Commons, the Whigs becoming more and more ' Conservative,' relying on the Irish members to maintain them in office."

One evening, after all other guests had departed, Sir William Molesworth and Charles Buller remained late at our house, talking of the present aspect of affairs. " I will tell you what *we* are coming to, Grote," said Charles Buller. " In no very long time from this, you and I will have to ' tell' Molesworth."*

* In the month of March, Sir William Molesworth brought forward a motion of censure on the whole tenour of our Colonial administration. To this an amendment was moved by Lord Sandon, censuring the entire cabinet, though it was asserted that Sir Robert Peel disapproved of the step. The house divided on the amendment, and rejected it by

To fill in the picture which in the foregoing pages has been sketched, I will here insert a letter which, coming from an eminent city merchant, affords evidence of the " out-of-doors " Reformers holding the same opinions as those of Sir William Molesworth and ourselves, relative to the useless cry of " Union among Reformers!" The writer, Mr. John Travers, well known as a leading political worker in the Radical interest, alludes in the letter to the projected grand dinner in Drury Lane Theatre, at which all Liberals were expected to appear.

" January 19th, 1837.

" Dear Madam,

" I shall endeavour to wait upon you on Saturday, but if unable to do so, I hope to be able to find you out, and to pay my respects to you at Drury Lane Theatre on Monday. " Of course I feel much interested about public affairs at this moment. . . Sir William Molesworth has done *great good*—Raikes Currie also. . . . I am sure you will forgive me, and so will Mr. Grote, when I say that Mr. Grote is a little *too passive*. A good stirring speech from him on Monday, however short, would do the cause and himself much good. I trust the opportunity will be afforded. If the meeting be not 'more Rad. than Whig,' it will do harm. I am not as yet satisfied of its propriety. I cannot give my support to Mr. Byng, or tolerate the thought of anything like cordial union (which this meeting seems to imply), if it be not one of more equality than in times past. And it is what we are entitled to, for I am sure that Radical opinions are spreading, and that the Whigs are getting weaker year by year. . . But the Radicals must, as soon as possible, form a party. They will be nothing without it. Take care that Mr. Hume is kept well in advance. He has great power in the country. I think sometimes I see him temporizing a little. Sir William Molesworth will else put him in the shade, and this should not be. With some agreed-upon plan, between a few such men (in which Mr. Grote is perfectly indispensable),

a majority of 29. Of the Radical Band, three individuals alone quitted the House without voting either way—viz., Mr. Grote, Sir William, and Mr. Leader; the two last being the mover and seconder of the original motion.

we must move on ; but we must not be deterred by the thought
of Tory invasion—this is a mere Whig cry to keep themselves
in place, and it is a risque—though hardly worth the name of
a risque—which we must encounter. Believe me,

" Very respectfully yours,

(Signed) "JOHN TRAVERS."

The grand demonstration took place on the stage
of Drury Lane, in January. It proved a mere Whig
affair, as was anticipated, and no more need be said
about it.

CHAPTER V.

1837. GENERAL ELECTION, ON DEATH OF KING WILLIAM THE FOURTH.—LETTERS CONCERNING ELECTION.—CITY OF LONDON CONTEST.—MR. GROTE'S ELECTION CARRIED BY SIX VOTES ONLY.

IN the early part of this year (1837) I received a letter from Molesworth, dictated with some acerbity it is true, but replete with hearty zeal for "the good cause," as it used to be termed amongst our party. I wish I could insert the whole letter here, but it is too long—the following are extracts :—

"Telcot (North Devon), January, 1837.

"I do not like Leeds—the Whigs want to make conditions with me about supporting ministers. I shall go there, however, if the roads are practicable. I think I can do good, and can rally round me a fierce party. . . .

"I assure you I am becoming very tired of Politics, and shall be heartily glad when I can get a little rest. . . .

"It is wished that I should be at the dinner to Morpeth, and that I should not fall very foul of ministers. I can do this tolerably well by talking about Ireland—feeling in England towards that country, &c., and conclude with 'Ballot.' What think you ? . . .

"Parkes, Rintoul, &c., are for my standing for Westminster on my own bottom. They think I could be returned. What say you ? If you should see Place, talk to him. . . . .

"My political conduct in the House next session will suit the Westminster Rads. Let me hear your opinion, and those of Warburton, &c., upon all subjects. Parkes's letter was truly *à la Parkes.* I like his comparing the Whig Government to the boiler of a steam-engine! In truth, it is

more like a tin-kettle with a hole in its bottom—fit neither to
boil fish nor flesh. . . .

"Keep Charles Buller straight. He acted like a man last
session at the close. I put him four times into my ' Article.' *
I like puffing my friends when I can.

"William Molesworth."

Politics grew rather worse than better, from the
Radical point of view, during the first half of 1837.
The endeavour to form what we termed a Radical
"brigade," of which the direction was destined for
Mr. Grote, failed, and in this manner:

The names of the members who had agreed to enrol
themselves in this section had been gradually collected,
by the active promoters of the movement, in a quiet
way; and the scheme was ripe for completion, when
Mr. Joseph Hume indiscreetly let out the secret to
O'Connell. That acute politician was instantly alive
to the danger to which such an organization of the
" philosophical Radicals" would lead, by withstanding
the Whig ministry, which he in his heart desired to
maintain in power. He adroitly adopted an effectual
means of tripping us up, by proposing to join the
" brigade," along with his Irish followers. Hume fell
into the trap, and exultingly communicated the wish
of O'Connell to the Radical chiefs. These wiser men
at once saw, in the suggestion, a death-blow to the
plan. They knew full well that if O'Connell came
into the party he would stultify its utility, assume
the management, and, by the numerical force of his
" contingent," turn the brigade into a powerless, perhaps a discredited, fraction of the House of Commons.
Messrs. Strutt and Hawkins were the first to " declare
off;" and this scheme, which, in its original form,
promised to strengthen the influence of sincere Reformers, fell through altogether. I have by me a
list of the members' names who were to have com-

* In the *London Review*.

posed the brigade; it comprises almost all the independent and pronounced Liberals then in Parliament.

The Session of 1837 came to a somewhat premature close by the death (in June) of the king, William IV. We had established our residence in Eccleston Street in the autumn of 1836; and our first season in London, in 1837, was a very hospitable one, many interesting foreign visitors coming over, to whom we felt bound to show attentions. Sir William Molesworth was a constant guest at our house, dividing his serious occupations between attendance at the House of Commons, and sharing in the conduct of his " Review," along with its editor, John S. Mill.

In July, 1837, Lord Durham judged it expedient to put forth a sort of *confession de foi* in a letter to a friend, Mr. Bowlby. It had the effect of entirely dissipating such hopes as his previous connexion with the Radicals had given birth to, of his willingness to put himself at the head of that party. At the same time, Lord Durham pretty surely closed the door of the cabinet against himself, because he was, now, formidable no longer. When he broke with his Radical " following," he could easily be kept out, and no one of the ministers was sorry that he should be kept out. Most of the Radicals felt hurt and angry at Lord Durham's " bid " for place, but neither Mr. Grote nor I were of this mind, not having expected any real or consistent support to Radical Politics from that wayward nobleman.* One day, early in

* I insert here letter from Francis Place to Mrs. Grote in connexion with this passage :—

16, Charing Cross,
January 2, 1839.

" . . . Lord Durham is a ' lost mutton.' He had a chance such as few men have had, but he was all a lord and none a man, and could not take the high station offered to him. He has found his place, which is indeed low enough, even among men who are far from high. . . .

" He is defunct as a public man, for henceforth no public man can

D

July, I received a note from Sir William which ran thus:—

"You cannot but suppose that I am in the deepest despair at not having seen you for so long. Will you ride to-day, and at what time? I must go to the House, and can't get away till about four o'clock. Or shall I drive you in my Tilbury? I want to talk to you about Lord Durham's *infamous* letter.

"Yours,

"W. M."

In connexion with the conduct of the Radicals at this juncture, I append here an extract from a letter of Mr. John Stuart Mill to myself, dated May, 1837:—

"What you say of W. accords with my expectations. I consider him, with his crotchettiness, and his fussiness, and his go-between inclinations, to be the evil genius of the Radical party. . . . He is 'out of my books,' as completely as Strutt and the rest of the pseudo-Radicals who voted for the extinction of popular government in Canada."

1837.—Parliament was dissolved in July. The "rout" of the Liberals at the elections was signal, but Sir William managed to obtain a seat for Leeds.

Mr. Grote carried his election for the City of London by a majority of six votes only; a dead set having been made against him by the Tories, who split votes for the other Liberal candidates, and thereby threw him to the bottom of the poll.*

be eminent who has not the people at his back. . . . I am upon the whole well pleased that the people of Devonport addressed him, as this led to the proceedings in Westminster, which brought him out, and showed that he could not occupy the place he was expected to fill. I am sorry he is so utterly incompetent, but it is well to know the fact at once. Not *one* body has addressed him, I believe, since the publication of the Westminster correspondence; he was let fall quietly— and there he lies. It is a very good symptom that the people so readily and so fully understand such things. . . ."

* Here is a portion of a letter written by me to Sir William (then at Leeds), dated City, 24th July, 1837, 5 p.m., being the final day of polling for the City election.

"I fear all is up with your friend Grote, this turn. Our committee affect to say we have a majority of 23 over Horsley Palmer. But, as

Whilst Mr. Grote and myself were on a tour in Switzerland, I received a letter from a friend closely mixed up with the political world. I extract a few passages.

August 17th.—" You will have seen how the Counties have been gained by the Tories, to such an extent; and with such facility, as if an epidemic had infected them all. The return of ' Old Glory' (Sir F. Burdett) for Wiltshire was especially disgraceful. But indeed, throughout all England, the spectacle has been disgraceful. Such venality and corruption in the old Boroughs, and intimidation in the Counties! Good must come out of evil however, and the necessity for the ballot has been made apparent to many men who have been hitherto opposed to it. . . .

" It is a melancholy prospect, but there are rays of hope which pierce through the gloom. The Radical band, although deprived of some of its chiefs, is not diminished in numbers, and the Government will be dependent on the English ' Rads,' who may therefore stipulate for conditions of alliance favourable to freedom. . . . My private opinion is that they (the Whigs) will lean to Toryism rather than to Radicalism. In truth there is little difference between the two aristocratic parties as to the principles of government, and the possession of place is almost the only ground of strife. We are then, I think, destined to ' grovel on' for a period, &c. . . . What a farce it is! Oh the contemptible rage for titles and ribands which I see! Thanks for the good laugh you gave me about Lord B. What an impostor he is! Why, last year he exerted himself with the Government to prevent the ballot being left an open question. . . . &c. &c.

"(T. Y.)"

we always find the sheriff's reckoning below that of the candidates' committees, we can hardly build upon it. At two o'clock to-day Palmer was 74 ahead of Grote. At three o'clock we had pulled this down to 30. To-morrow, at one o'clock, we shall know our fate.

" Everybody is ' consternated!' I am *composed* and *resigned*, and, bearing in mind your strenuous objections, I did *not cry* at seeing G. just now address the enormous crowd in Guildhall, dubious whether he was their representative. I now look to *your* return as the only one I feel much interest in. Parkes is in the city, looking horribly ' down,' and croaking like an old hoarse crow. Good-bye!

(Signed)   " H. G.

" Sir W. Molesworth, Bart.,
          Leeds."

1837.—Sir William did not come up from Cornwall to attend the meeting of the new Parliament, which took place in November. In those days a journey from Pencarrow to London was a serious affair; no railway communication being established on the western line, posting was Sir William's customary mode of travelling to and from the metropolis. I received a letter from him in October, 1837, of which that which follows is a copy.

"Pencarrow, Oct. 1837.

. . . " I have been leading a life of placid repose and tranquillity—devoid of all worldly cares. Leader came here about the beginning of September; so did Trelawny, &c., and we have in consequence had a very agreeable and sensible party. Charles Buller was here likewise. He is more Whiggish than ever. A pamphlet, once *puffed* by *Chronicle*, as of ministerial authority, then *abused* by that paper as being too servile, is said by some to be written by Charles. I only know that he agrees with it. . . . Your political gloom I don't share in. I think the Whigs are miserable wretches, and shall rejoice when I hear their death shriek, and shall look with pleasure on their death agony. I have a firm faith in the progress of the human mind, and in the steady advance of democracy, and don't believe the Whigs can keep us back. We, who are in immediate contact with them, and see how loathsome they are, are revolted and disgusted. . . . The people are moderate Radicals, and their eyes can't and wont be opened to the acts of the Whigs.

" You ask what I have been about for the cause? why, I have been very lazy, and reading only for pleasure. Leader brought me a work on Probabilities, by Poisson, and I could not resist the temptation of reading it and returning for a time to my mathematical lore. I am now busily engaged digesting my report upon Transportation, which is hard work; but I hope it wont take above a hundred folio pages, as I can say a great deal in a little space. I have at last established a secretary, and find him most useful. . . . We shall not return to town till just before the meeting of Parliament, when we shall commence our establishment in your vicinity, if our house is ready. . . . I have nothing further to say except that Mill writes me a capital account of the next number of the *London*. There are to be two articles by himself; one on ' Armand

Carrel and French Politics,' which he thinks is the best thing he ever wrote; and one on our 'Politics.' I cordially agree with him in the opinions he has stated to me on the subject.

"Best regards to Grote. Write to me soon.

"W. MOLESWORTH."

My letters to Sir William, in return, were of a varied character. Along with the political news and gossip I permitted myself, as the privileged friend, to administer therein many a good scold for his rude and uncourteous habits. Here is one extract from a letter of mine dated Oct. 1837.

"As you *are* engaged on the study of 'Probabilities,' I wish you would make a calculation of the chances of your ever becoming a civilized being. For my own part, I think you had better let me negociate with Mr. Audubon to take you out to Illinois with him next March, and make a 'Partie' for you, with the daughter of one of the Sioux chiefs, with a dowry of hunting grounds, eh?"

Another of about the same period, 1837, on our return from a tour in Switzerland :—

"Got your homily. Deuced dull concern. Daresay you are wondrous clever at 'Horoscoping' down there in your old library; but we worldlings don't take it in exactly the same light. We think politics mighty gloomy. . . . Write to me soon *if* you have recovered from your fit of the 'grumps.'

(Signed)   "H. G."

Again, in October, 1837, London, I wrote thus :—

"The *Pencarrow Dispatch* 'took the shine' out of both *Morning Post* and *Gazette* this morning (the latter a new 'launch' of Travers's); couldn't get on with my breakfast for laughing thereat. Grote and Roebuck, who were quarrelling like dog and cat over Webster's Speeches, were quieted by my reading out some of your letter, at which G. laughed immoderately, but at no passage more than at your blood being put up about Raikes Currie's rival 'letter.' I have sent for said R. C. to bring me the epistle, and will, according to your wish, 'well and truly try and a true verdict give.' . . .

" I rejoice to say that, on our return hither (from a visit to the Bullers at Englefield Green), we found Roebuck much better. He had heated G.'s library up to about 75°, got down a single vol. of a dozen different works, which were strewn, open, about the room. Sofa tumbled into a hammock; ' Toronto Independents' and Canadian Crackers filled each table; ink and pens used up, and *he* sound asleep when we arrived, *Spectator* in one hand, *Thiers* in the other. Perfectly happy and no pain. . . . G. is ' doing' nothing, save writing to country balloteers, and reading to *amuse himself.* He is very well, and he laughed at C. Buller's jokes till he cried again. He laughed, however, almost as much at *his own* against Charles; appearing to believe C. to be the author of the *Domestic Prospects:* ' as Charles says in his able pamphlet,' and, ' as the acute author of the pamphlet* observes,' and so on, much to Buller's annoyance and our amusement. Buller is *not* however gone Whiggish. He and I had a long serious ' confab' on Friday evening, when he rehearsed a famous speech for the ' address' night, which I bet him he would never have the courage to deliver.† What say you ? . . .

"I should not be so kind and indulgent (?) as I am, but that I hear you so abused, and this makes me take fire and defend you. But I have never got *farther* into the actual complaints against you than that you are insolent, rude, and vain. To which defects I own, on your behalf, but add, that these qualities form the safeguard of your political virtue.

" O'Connell's letter to Roebuck signifieth ' funk' for the Whig lease of power. He retaineth him (Roebuck) for the Dublin election petition. We have letters from B——m again; Durham, I trust, is ' laid in the Red Sea,' as a declared humbug. . . . Mrs. Buller means to attend your *soirées*, and thinks that between you both (*i.e.*, Mr. Leader) half a dozen more women may be prevailed upon to come; but among them do not rely on your humble servant. . . .

" Well, good-bye ! glad to see that my (agreeable) letters have smoothed your rugged brow.

"H. G."

---

* The same as that alluded to in page 36 by Sir W. Molesworth.
† I should have lost, as it turned out.

CHAPTER VI.

1837, 1838.   MR. GROTE'S VIEW OF THE "SITUATION" OF
POLITICAL AFFAIRS. — THE CANADA REBELLION. — SIR
WILLIAM MOLESWORTH PROPOSES TO EDIT THE WORKS
OF THOMAS HOBBES.—PARIS PROJECT.   ABANDONED ON
ACCOUNT OF ILLNESS.—LETTERS FROM MRS. GROTE TO
SIR WILLIAM MOLESWORTH.

PARLIAMENT met in November.   The Whigs had got
"fresh legs" by the accession and popularity of the
new monarch, who thought fit to keep them in their
places.   Thus, notwithstanding the losses of seats by
their own partizans, they managed, by the aid of
O'Connell, and by the not unwilling support of Sir
Robert Peel, to maintain their ground, and to defy
their Radical allies.   Lord John Russell "threw off"
in fact, with a distinct declaration against further
reform, in a speech which afterwards got him the name
of "Finality John."   On this occasion, Mr. Charles
Buller, with a courage that did him honour, defended
the principles of progress, whilst he cast reproach upon
Lord John for deserting those colours under which
he and his friends had risen to power.   A prodigious
Civil List was proposed for the young Queen, and
opposed by the Radicals.   A committee was ultimately appointed, in 1838, to consider the Civil List,
and another to inquire into the Pension List, on both
of which Mr. Grote served: being supported, on
occasion, by his brother Radicals, George Evans and
E. Strutt.

1838.—The Government's resolutions referring to the war in Canada, in the Session of 1838, caused great dissatisfaction among the Radical members. Mr. Grote took a prominent part in opposing and denouncing their policy at every turn, sustained by Mr. Hume, Mr. Warburton, Roebuck and Molesworth, chiefly. The main body of the Liberals, however, sided with the Whigs, and the minorities representing the Radical party came to be exceedingly slender, sometimes reaching no greater amount than sixteen, or even nine votes.

As affording a confirmation of Molesworth's impressions concerning the futility of Radical efforts in Parliament, I venture to introduce here an extract from a letter written by Mr. Grote to his friend John Austin, bearing date February, 1838.*

"The Whig Government has been, ever since the accession of our present Queen, becoming more and more confirmed in its Conservative tendencies; in fact it is now scarcely at all distinguished either in its leanings or its acts from Peel and his friends. . . .

"Lord Melbourne's majority is a very inconsiderable one, and he maintains himself in the Ho. of Commons chiefly by making use of the Radicals against the Tories, and of the Tories against the Radicals. If by any accident these two should be united in a vote upon a question of importance, his ministry must be demolished. . . .

"A few years' enjoyment of power and patronage has inspired the present Ministry and their supporters with all those faults which used to be the exclusive attributes of the Tories. Little or nothing would be lost by the accession to power of Sir Rob. Peel just now, and this at least would be gained—that we should then have a respectable popular opposition. . . .

"You of course are familiar with the peremptory declaration made by Lord John Russell on the first day of the Session, proclaiming the absolute finality of the Reform Act, declaring war against Ballot, Triennial Parliaments, and any extension of the suffrage. . . . The affairs of Canada

* Mr. Austin was at this time employed on the inquiry into the condition of the Maltese, along with Mr. George Cornewall Lewis.

have turned out most calamitous: the discontents in Lower Canada were so bitterly aggravated by the resolutions passed by the English Parliament last spring, that there has been open rebellion, and the Ministry have been driven to propose further measures of coercion against that colony, resisted by some fifteen Radicals in the Ho. of Commons, amongst whom I was one. But Peel compelled them to drink some bitter cups of humiliation during the passing of their bill for suspending the Canadian Constitution. . . .

"The degeneracy of the Liberal party and their passive acquiescence in everything, good or bad, which emanates from the present Ministry, puts the accomplishment of any political good out of the question, and it is not at all worth while to undergo the fatigue of a nightly attendance in Parliament for the simple purpose of sustaining *Whig* Conservatism against *Tory* Conservatism. I now look wistfully back to my unfinished Greek History. I hope the time will soon arrive when I can resume it. The expenses of defending my seat are furnished by a subscription among the electors, to which I and my colleagues contribute 100*l.* each, and no more. I set so little value on my seat, personally, that I doubt whether I should attempt to defend it at my own expense. . . . Toryism is regaining its ascendancy, and we must before long have a thorough Tory Ministry; even that will be a slight improvement, rather than otherwise, upon our present state, when we have both a Conservative Ministry and a Conservative opposition.

> "Believe me,
> > "My dear Austin,
> > > "Yours faithfully,
> > > (Signed) "Geo. Grote."

On more than one occasion, during the years 1835-1836, I had suggested to Sir William that he would confer a benefit on the students of political philosophy by bringing out an edition of the works of Thomas Hobbes of Malmsbury; adding thereto a preface, which should give an appreciation of the various writings and speculative disquisitions of that profound thinker. The notion fell in with Sir William's turn of mind, and on reflection he said he would endeavour to carry it out. Accordingly he engaged a literary assistant to prepare the text, and, at the point of time my narrative now treats of, the edition was actually in progress, Sir William intending to occupy himself with the critical essay so soon as he should have completed his " Report" on Transportation.* At this stage of his undertaking, Sir William addressed the following letter to Mr. Grote :—

"Bodmin, Sept. 27, 1838.

" My dear Grote,

" Having determined to publish an edition of the works of Hobbes, I write to ask permission to dedicate them to you, as a testimony of my admiration and regard.

" I send you a list of the contents of the volumes in the order I propose to publish them, commencing however with the second ; the life will be published last. The 2nd, 3rd, 4th, and 5th vols. of the English, and the 10th, 11th, 12th Latin works, will be most admirable books, worthy to be studied by all imbued with a philosophic spirit. It is with the advice of C. Austin, who, having once intended to publish an edition of Hobbes, has carefully considered the subject, that I have determined upon the arrangement of the volumes.

" I should feel excessively obliged to you, if you have any observation to make upon the best mode of publishing these works, if you would favour me with your advice and assistance. It will, I think, take between three and four years to bring out the whole work, during which period the study of Hobbes' works, necessary to the publication of them, will, I trust, render it easy for me to write his life and a view of his philosophy.

" I am sorry to hear that you have been unwell, particularly at this period, when alone there has been any fine weather. I hope that you are quite recovered. My health is somewhat better. In the political world there seems to me to be nothing of any interest. O'Connell's Letters are particularly stupid,

---

* To this latter question he had long directed his attentive study, expounding his views in Parliament and in his Review with considerable skill and power. Indeed, both his speeches and his " report" were ultimately considered by all parties as exhibiting the most instructive and thoroughly effectual treatment hitherto applied to that thorny subject.

and in some respects disgusting. I am afraid there is no immediate prospect of any good, and I am very tired of the wearisome broils of political life.

"Believe me, yours truly,

(Signed) "WM. MOLESWORTH."

About this period Mr. Grote and I had contemplated going over to Paris for a week or two, as a recreative excursion, and Sir William having asked to be allowed to join the party, he writes as follows :—

"Pencarrow, Sept. 1838.

. . . "I shall be at your orders about the 17th Nov., but remember I am to be *with you;* lodgings or hotel, I don't care which, but I wont be separated. . . . I am, as you know, not a marrying man : I have other things to do, among which the most important is my edition of Hobbes. C. Austin and myself have been discussing this subject with great interest. He intended once to undertake it himself, and has given me much useful information. . . . I have written to-day to Mr. Grote to ask permission to dedicate the volumes to him. I wish for that permission for two reasons—1. Because I shall ever feel the deepest gratitude for the philosophical instruction he gave me when I first knew him, which induced me to study Hobbes and similar authors, and created a taste in my mind for that style of reading. 2. Because I have a greater regard and esteem for himself and his wife than for any other people in this wicked world. . . . Why should I pay you 10*l.*?* first, how can you prove I owe you anything ? secondly, you ought to pay *me,* for all the amusement I have afforded you. However, when we are in Paris I don't mind if I do make you a present, to clear off all scores," &c. &c.

"27th Sept. 1838.

. . . "The 1st vol. of Hobbes will come last, so that I shall have had all the benefit of perusing and reperusing, studying and restudying Hobbes in the correction of the proofs, &c. It will be not much less than a four years' work, and in that time I may produce something not very bad, in the shape of a 'Life,' &c."

* This is an allusion to a standing joke between us about a debt to me which Sir William never would repay.

Mr. Grote to Sir W. Molesworth.

"Threadneedle Street, October 2nd, 1838.

"My dear Molesworth,

"Your letter respecting your project of editing Hobbes' works reached me at Burnham on Sunday. I cannot but feel flattered, as well as pleased, at the wish which you express to dedicate it to me, and I most willingly consent that you should do so. Our poor friend and instructor, old Mill — *utinam viveret !—he* was the man to whom such a dedication would have been more justly due. . . .

"In one respect I am a very fit person to have the work dedicated to me; for I take a warm and anxious interest in its completion and success,—not less from my esteem and friendship for the editor than from my admiration of the author edited. If there are any points on which you desire my advice or co-operation, be assured that it will give me sincere pleasure to afford it. You have got a copious and lofty subject, affording scope for every variety of intellectual investigation—embracing morals, politics, and metaphysics, and including even the English civil war and the Restoration. It is worthy of the most capacious intellect, as well as of the most unremitting perseverance, and I trust that you will devote labour enough to enable you to do it full justice.

"Have you read Comte's ' Traité de Philosophie Positive,' of which a third volume has just been published ? It seems a work full of profound and original thinking, and will be of service to you when you come to appreciate the physical and mathematical orbit of Hobbes. I am sorry to say, however, that I do not find in it the solution of those perplexities respecting the fundamental principles of geometry, which I have never yet been able to untie to my own satisfaction. Nor can I at all tolerate the unqualified manner in which he strikes out morals and metaphysics from the list of positive sciences.

"The other day at the Athenæum I took up one of the volumes of the ' Documens pour servir à l'Histoire de France,' which I found to be the production of Victor Cousin, and to relate to the philosophy of the Middle Ages, during the age of Abelard and Roscellinus. There are some clear and instructive reflections in it on the controversy of that day between the Nominalists and Realists. It appears that some new MSS. of Abelard have recently been found, which throw light upon the question as it was then argued.

"Our contemporary politics are in a state of profound

slumber, from which I fear they are not likely to awake, except to cause us disgust and discouragement. There is nothing in them fit to occupy the attention of a common-place but sincere patriot, much less of a philosopher.

" I congratulate you on having fixed upon a subject which will give you steady intellectual occupation. Sure I am, by my own experience as well as from all other considerations, that you will be much the happier for it.

" Believe me, my dear Molesworth,
" Yours very faithfully,
(Signed) " GEO. GROTE."

"Sir W. Molesworth, Bart., M.P.''

To those who knew Sir W. Molesworth only after the year 1844, the following passage of a letter of mine may perhaps be read with surprise. I insert it as affording an insight into his habits of behaving in former times. It bears date August, 1838 :—

" Charles Austin was with us on Sunday at East Burnham, with which place he professes himself ravished, and threatens frequent visits after his return.

" Last week we spent an evening at John Austin's. Mrs. Buller there. Austin in good cue ; talked about you ; wish you had heard us ! how you would have laughed ! Nothing could divest Austin of the error of supposing that you desired to be liked and esteemed. Arguing over and over that you should not do this, that, and the other, *for* 'that it was not the way to gain people's good-will,' &c., &c., I, as often, assuring him that there was nothing you desired *so little* as ' to gain people's good opinion ;' that you distinctly avowed strong objections to being ' liked ;' preferred being *dis*liked ; ' only aimed at being feared,' and so on.

" Austin, staring me in the face, shoving pinches of snuff up his nostrils, and hesitating to accredit my asseverations. Ma'am Buller, *sniggering* on the sofa, observed that ' you certainly succeeded extremely well in preventing the growth of " likings,"' &c. John Austin is fond of you, in spite of all your absurd 'goings on,' and he and I heartily deplored and admired in concert, and in the same direction. Everybody seems to hold *me* in some sort accountable for your 'sau-vagerie,' and pretends to think I encourage your follies by

laughing at them, though I tell them I have long since abandoned the office of censor. . . . As to our Paris project,
'entre nous,' I think it will *come off* as sure as you're a
sinner (not *I*), about middle of November.

"H. G."

Mrs. Grote to Sir W. Molesworth.

"4th October, 1838.

. . . "I look forward to much agreeable 'fid fad,' gossip,
and amusement during our Paris *slant*, among the various
sources of which will be that of observing you in a new
character, playing at 'spectable!' . . . Grote and I talk
about your 'opus magnum' with much interest. You will do
yourself much honour if you acquit yourself well of this undertaking, which I, for one, have good faith in your doing. I
do hope that you will live to rear a reputation worth having,
and that you will cease to impair its usefulness by your
farouche, misanthropic demeanour, which never can answer
any good purpose, while it excites angry passions in other
people." . . .

1838.—When the time drew near for realizing the
Paris project, Sir William unfortunately fell ill, and
his medical adviser set himself earnestly against his
patient's leaving home at the threshold of winter.
Accordingly Sir William relinquished his purpose of
accompanying Mr. Grote and myself to Paris, and we
set forth without him. We felt disappointed at losing
his company on this jaunt, but his health was regarded by us as of such paramount importance that
we could not but approve of his prudence in renouncing his design of taking this holiday in the
month least favourable for travelling.

Here is a part of one of my letters written to Sir
William on learning this decision :—

Mrs. Grote to Sir W. Molesworth.

"4, Eccleston Street, London,
"October 24th, 1838.

. . . "Mrs. Austin prophesied a 'brouille' between us
before a fortnight should elapse. She vowed that I should

never tolerate you as a ' familiar' more than a week, notwithstanding the suavity of my temper; she is therefore full of congratulations to me at my being ' shot of you.' . . . George says he is reconciled to the disappointment by the excellent use you will make of your time ; and, in fact, no one can blame you for taking care of a health proved to be so liable to danger under changes of temperature. . . .

" Roebuck called on G. lately, and gave us a long ' yarn about Canada. For the first time in his life *he* is in the dumps about general politics. He read G. great part of a letter from poor Papineau, by which we learn that Lord D. has wholly alienated the French party, who hold him in aversion and mistrust. You and I never did augur any good from Lord D.'s mission, and so I am not disappointed. I am only enraged at the subjugation of that province by a huge military force, which for the time annihilates all *hope* of further rebellion. I saw Mrs. Jamieson lately, who was in Upper Canada a week before the outbreak of last October. She gives the same account as R. does of the feeling towards Lord D. there. She is favourable to Papineau's party, but thinks the game is up for this turn. Alas ! . . . G. and I think the old spelling of Hobbes should be used in your new edition, as far as consists with entire perspicuity. . . . We are in town for a day or two, and have summoned all who are in town to come to us on Friday. Austins of course, Lewis, some New Yorkers, Bullers, Dr. Arnott, Joe Parkes, C. Austin, Alfred Austin, Sharpe, and so on, Mr. McDuffie (member of Congress); also . . ."

The summer of 1839 was consumed by attendance on an election petition from the borough of Carlow. Mr. Grote was named chairman of the committee, and he attended daily morning sittings in the House of Commons, in the discharge of this duty, for the space of eleven weeks—Sundays of course excepted. The attendance at the evening debate being added to the former, it may be easily conceived that little leisure was available for recreation or society. Mr. Grote was scarcely a night absent from London for many months; and although we had now established our residence at " Burnham Beeches," it was scarcely of any use to us, as I did not think it right to leave

Mr. Grote for more than a day or two at a time to enjoy this summer retreat. During the latter part of August, and the whole of September, Mr. Grote was in close attendance at his banking-house, his partner taking a holiday for this season.

In the autumn we left England, and, after an interesting tour in Belgium, visiting the principal cities and monuments, spent some months in Paris. Thus it comes to be explained how that we saw less of Molesworth during the greater part of 1839.

The political struggles about Canada had, at this period, sensibly loosened the bond of union among the Radical party, only a few showing a decided resistance to the Government measures for coercing the Canadian people.

Mr. Grote brought on his motion for taking votes by ballot on the 18th of June of this year; but though he sustained it with his accustomed ability and fervour, the debate was confessedly dull and languid, and few or none came to congratulate me on Grote's performance—a fact indicative of how altered a feeling had come over the Liberals in the House. On previous occasions the Radical members were wont to come to our house and pour out their exultation at the success of the speech and the promise of progress which the debate afforded.

CHAPTER VII.

1840, 1841.   VISIT   TO   PENCARROW.—DISAPPOINTMENT   IN
LOVE   SUIT.—CORRESPONDENCE.

SIR WILLIAM had frequently indicated a wish to see
Mr. Grote and myself at Pencarrow. But the few
opportunities which were then afforded to Mr. Grote
of taking recreative excursions, left us little time for
visiting far-distant friends. In the summer of 1840,
I went to pass a few days with the Rev. Sydney
Smith and his family, at his parsonage, Combe-Florey,
in Somersetshire, taking with me in my postchaise
Mrs. Anna Jameson, the accomplished authoress.
Sir William wrote to me at Combe-Florey to press my
coming on to Pencarrow (being already a hundred
and fifty miles on the way), and I was disposed to
consent, when circumstances arose which induced
Mr. Grote to request my speedy return home. Finding Sir William exceedingly disappointed by my
failing him in August, I prevailed on Mr. Grote to
arrange for both of us to pay a visit to Cornwall in
the following October. We accordingly quitted our
residence at Burnham Beeches, and posted down by
easy journeys all the way to Pencarrow, where we
arrived, I think, in the afternoon of the fourth day.
My health was so delicate that I could not bear more
than eight hours' travelling without suffering from
headache of painful amount, even though we jour-

neyed in a comfortable, easy postchaise, rolling along with four horses all the way.

We found Sir William in very fair health, and much delighted to receive us, for the first time, *chez-lui*. Lady Molesworth (his mother) and Miss Mary Molesworth were residing with him, according to their wont at this season. We had not been at Pencarrow many days, when Sir William invited me, early one forenoon, to hearken to the recital of his former life—from boyhood upwards.

We sat down in a small *salon* looking out upon a beautiful garden, and he entered upon the subject without the smallest reserve. I never interrupted him, and he must have spoken from three-quarters of an hour to an hour. " I was," he said, " a weakly child, and was sent quite early in my boyhood to a private boarding-school near London (at Chelsea, I think he said), where I was ill cared for, and but negligently taught. My father disliked me, and never wished to be troubled with the sight of me. My mother took more interest in me, but while my father, Sir Arscott, lived, she could not do so much for me as she would otherwise have done. I was afflicted with 'King's Evil' (in plain English), insomuch that my whole throat, ears, and neck, were ulcerated, and one of my ears was all but obliterated by this cruel disease, for which— strange as it may seem to you to learn it — no medical treatment was invoked; my schoolfellows made sport of me, and allowed themselves to use language which cut me to the soul, in reference to my deplorable infirmity. When my father died, my mother bestowed a great deal more care upon me, and my bodily health becoming improved by judicious management, I began to address myself seriously to study, for which I had a natural leaning, but it derived additional force from the incapacity for mixing in youthful exercises and pastimes under which I laboured. My mother placed me in Germany, under the care of a Dr. Bekker, living near Frankfort, an able and conscientious preceptor, where I remained for some time; after which I was entered at the University of Cambridge, and attended to my studies—especially mathematics—to which science I felt strongly attracted indeed, and might possibly have distinguished myself therein. However, my career as a member of the university was interrupted in its second year, owing to a quarrel which arose between my tutor and myself, in which I considered myself ill-treated, and accordingly sent the gentleman a regular challenge, to fight me with pistols. I crossed over to Calais, and awaited my adversary where the law could not interpose between us. (I am sorry to say that my memory fails me here, as to whether the tutor followed Sir William over the Channel or not.) The consequence of this sally of youthful imprudence was, a decree of expulsion from the university of which I was a member.

" My mother hereupon decided that my education should be resumed under the professors of the University of Edinburgh, whither she removed her residence, about the year 1828, taking with her my two sisters. After I had gone through my academical course of study there, which I did with considerable zeal and interest, I felt a lively inclination for a taste of pleasure and enjoyment, and, on the verge of my majority, broke away for the south of Europe, with health and strength enough for some youthful follies and vanities, and yet not enough to lead me entirely away from serious pursuits. Your kinsman, John Charles Dundas, once informed you, I recollect, how that I united the course of a young votary of pleasure with the steady cultivation of letters. He, with several more Englishmen, was at Naples at the same time with myself, and they used to wonder at my shutting myself up for several hours in the morning, with my Arabic professor, with whom I was learning more than one Oriental language, having a floating notion of taking a journey to the East at no very distant day.

"Whilst revelling in my freedom, and in the enjoyment of life's choicest blessings, in Italy, news reached me of the movement going forward in the English political world (the offshoot of the Revolution of July, 1830, and of the Duke of Wellington's emphatic denial of all Reform of Parliament). My friends conjured me to return, representing in forcible language the obligation I lay under of joining the Liberal cause at so critical a juncture, the chance of my carrying an election as member for Cornwall if I were on the spot, the encouragement my presence would afford to my tenantry to exert themselves, &c. &c. Not to dilate upon all these points, I took the resolution of returning to England. It was a step prompted by a sense of duty, and that alone. Renouncing my purposes of travel, I plunged into public turmoil when my mind and character were only just maturing themselves, at a time when I had not yet had the means of contracting profitable connexions with superior persons: knowing but little of the ways of the world, and little fitted for it by disposition and tastes. However, I regarded it as a duty to come forward in my native county, my birth and station constituting a certain claim to the representation of that county: to contest which, moreover, an ample fortune, over which I had just acquired the control, supplied me the *pecuniary* power.

"I returned, then, to my paternal home, suffered myself to be named as a candidate in the event of a general election, and my destiny was cast from that hour in the form under which you have known me, and have been associated with me, for the whole period succeeding the Reform Bill. My Radical opinions,

himself that she regarded him with interest, possibly with favour. His fancy magnified the indications, perhaps, but I believe that Miss T—— did entertain a certain partiality for her admirer, she being a girl capable of recognising and esteeming those intellectual gifts, and that force of character of which even his detractors could not deny to him the possession.

In the afternoon of the next day but one, I was sitting quietly in the drawing-room by myself, when in came Sir William, his face flushed with emotion, and his voice tremulous and agitated.

"What is the matter, Sir William, I beg?" He took a glance round the drawing-rooms, to make sure that no one was within hearing, and then burst out—

" She is nothing but a —— heartless coquette! and I have lavished my affections on a cold, hard girl!"

He then recounted the incidents of the dinner at Sir Hussey Vivian's, with the sequel—viz., that buoyed up by the conversation at the dinner-table, Molesworth had joined the ladies at the earliest moment, and when, after a brief space, the whole family made a move to depart, Molesworth endeavoured to place her evening wraps around the shoulders of Miss T——, but that she abruptly took the shawl from his hands, and refused to permit it, or even to take his arm to the carriage.

When I heard this account, I was indeed incapable of offering any comfort to poor Molesworth. He stayed a long while, expatiating on the ill fortune which attended every love-pursuit of his—eating, and drinking champagne, storming against every member of the T—— family in turn, and winding up his philippic with " —— them all; they repudiate my attentions, and pretend to think me unworthy as a suitor! I will tell you what, my dear friend, I will marry my cook, and society shall be forced to swallow *her!* and I shall be revenged on them all, by ——."

After this decisive passage, I began to regard the case as next to hopeless. Poor Molesworth oscillated for awhile, however, between love and fury, and seemed irresolute how to act. Meanwhile, I would *not* consent to his making her a formal proposal. I said that without better grounds than were apparent to us for believing Miss T—— favourable to his passion, I could not suffer him to incur the risk of a fresh mortifying refusal, and consequently that of being laughed at by the sneerers of his acquaintance. As a final move, I took an opportunity of consulting Mr. Charles Buller (M.P. for Liskeard), an intimate acquaintance of ours, of Molesworth's, and of the young lady. "Do you think she likes him?" I asked. "Yes, I think she does." "Well, but if that should be the case, perhaps he would do well to come boldly forward as a candidate for her hand?" " No," replied C. Buller, "and I will explain to you why not. That family are very affectionately united. The girl respects and loves her father, and depend upon it she will never marry a man whom he dislikes and disapproves of, as he does Molesworth."

So I threw up the cards. Sir William made one last tentative, riding in the park one evening alongside of Miss T——. It failed of its purpose, and he took the wise, though painful determination of abandoning his pursuit.*

Mr. Grote and I left England in the autumn of 1841, and passed the winter in the south of Italy. I

* I afterwards came to know the real history of the dinner at Sir Hussey Vivian's, and may as well subjoin it here. During dinner, Mr. T—— noticed Sir William's earnest manner in conversing with his daughter; Mrs. T—— observed the disquiet brewing in her husband's mind, and in consequence felt uneasy in her turn. So, when the ladies retired, she administered an emphatic *avis* to her daughter, enjoining her to give no encouragement to Sir W'liam's attentions, *for* that it would displease Mr. T—— extremely. Moved by the parental admonition, she accordingly gave him the rebuff, as narrated above.

corresponded with Sir William during these months, and insert extracts from both my own and his letters.

Sir William Molesworth to Mr. Grote.

"Pencarrow, September, 1841.

"Why have you not written to me? what has become of you? where have you been? I am living a life of the most tranquil repose; reading mathematics, studying the undulatory theory of light, enjoying my garden when God permits— seldom enough however; seeing but few of the human brutes, contemning all of them; delighted at being free from the turmoil of politics; rejoicing at the annihilation of the Whigs, &c. &c.

"I have had much sport in rousing the indignation of the Tories in this county, by compelling them to an expensive contest, causing them to expend more thousands than we did hundreds, ...

"I have thus told you what I have done and am doing. Day succeeds to day, without other change than is marked by the successive pages in the books I am reading. What I am going to do, Providence alone is acquainted with. I am very happy as I am, and have no desire to change in any way." . . .

Mrs. Grote to W. Molesworth.

"Florence, October, 1841.

"I got your letter of last September, which portrayed a life of harmless recreation, unmarked by any of those fiercer impulses which have unhappily so often actuated you. I dread lest this blessed calm should not endure, for you seem destined to oscillate between *ennui* and fury; and I always live in fear of the latter phase coming to the upside after a certain *lull*. . . .

"I heartily pray that this fit of studious repose may be protracted, not *ad infinitum*, but *ad* my return, when I shall want a *listener* beyond any other object. You know you always laid claim to vast talents in that way, though I cannot say that I recognise them in their fullest extent, seeing that a really good listener ought not to allow long, awful yawns to escape him, such as, I regret to say, *have* occurred but too frequently during the course of my narrations to yourself."

Sir W. Molesworth to Mrs. Grote.

"Pencarrow, November 19, 1841.

" From nine to ten hours a day I occupy in reading. . . .

" *What* (you will ask) have I been reading? The positive sciences, to which each day I am becoming more devoted. In them alone can I find any semblance of certitude; in all the rest doubt, uncertainty, and presumptuous ignorance reign. I have been studying the undulatory theory of light in its latest form, beset with the greatest mathematical difficulties. I wish you were at Paris, in order that you might ask Arago some questions on the subject which I wish answered. Besides mathematics I have been reading Comte's last volume, with which I am very much pleased. Ask Grote how he likes it. Many of the views in it are very striking. The fundamental positions with regard to the historic development of the human race appear to me correct. Grote would consider them as too hopeful. I think not, but I am more sanguine than he is. How I should enjoy a conversation and discussion with him on the subject! I remember, with untiring delight, the visit of last year; and I hope I shall see you both again at Pencarrow, and hear him learnedly descant on Aristotle, the first of men, for whom with increase of knowledge one's admiration increases. At present I am reading the whole of Comte's work for the third time, with the determination of fully understanding every general proposition in the two first volumes—a task of great magnitude; for it will take me over the whole field of mathematics, geometry, mechanics, astronomy, light, and heat. The first volume and the three first sciences I have concluded, with the exception of the incidental perusal of the great work of Lagrange, with which I am now occupied. I begin to feel sometimes now that I am becoming a mathematician, and subjects which I formerly found difficult now appear easy. In short, I am conscious of mental progress, though, alas! not so rapid a one as I could wish. My object is not, however, to be a mathematician, but to imbue myself with the methods of investigating truth, so as to be a general thinker. For this purpose, and as a discipline of the mind, the rigorous study of some specific branch of knowledge is most beneficial, provided care be taken at the same time not to allow the methods of that particular science to obtain an undue preponderance over the intellect. I am well aware, better probably than most men, of the errors in philosophizing, into which mathematicians are apt to fall, and hope to escape them. In studying mathematics my object is not so much the conclusions arrived at by the great mathematicians, as the *methods* by which they arrived at them ; a study therefore not of mathematics, &c., but of the human mind about mathematics, &c. &c."

Then Sir William goes on to tell me that Miss T—— has been wooed and won by a young Cornish gentleman of his acquaintance, but he makes no comment upon the fact.

I return, for a space, to the political condition of affairs at the commencement of 1841. Parliament met in January, the Government being frequently subjected to humiliation, and even to defeat, in consequence of the augmented force of the Conservative party. The gain of several seats which fell vacant in the recess, of Nottingham and Sandwich, and others, completed the ascendancy of Sir Robert Peel, and emboldened him to adopt a line of aggressive policy against the Whig ministry. After a defeat on their Budget, Sir Robert moved a vote of want of confidence, or what was equivalent to one, and after several nights debating, the Tories carried the hostile resolution by a majority of one vote.

After this victory, the exultation of the Tories knew no bounds, and the speedy advent of their chief to the post of first Minister was expected. Still, the Whigs stuck to their places, and, as a last expedient, dissolved Parliament, in the month of June; trusting to a partial relaxation in our system of carrying on foreign trade, and a modification of the Corn Laws, to rally the Liberal party.

The experiment signally failed, and the Tories were reported to have acquired from sixty to seventy additional members.

When Parliament first met in January, 1841, Mr. Grote spoke on the debate on the Address, and it was almost the last occasion on which he thought it his duty to do so. The subject of our proceedings in reference to the Porte and the Viceroy of Egypt—commonly known as the Eastern Question, or *La Question de l'Orient*—being adverted to, Mr. Grote declared his strong dissatisfaction at the mode in which the Secretary for Foreign Affairs had managed the affair, and expressed deep regret at the irritation engendered in the minds of our French neighbours by our insolent behaviour in connexion with this question.

This speech made a lively impression upon all who listened to it, and led to a spirited debate, which would never have arisen but for Mr. Grote's able attack on the foreign Secretary's policy. In fact I remember no occasion on which he so well acquitted himself as an effective speaker on general subjects, as he did on this. The speech was admired for its elegance, its arrangement, its logical force, and for its manner of delivery. Among the persons who heard this earnest protest of a pacific private citizen against the high-handed conduct of the Foreign Office, was Mr. Samuel Jones Loyd, himself a good speaker, and a competent judge of oratory. He came to tell me how much pleasure it had given him to hear his old friend to such advantage, and ended his account of the impression made upon the house and upon his own mind, by saying " In fact I cannot conceive of anything superior to Grote's performance of this evening."

I mention this little passage, both because it affords a record of the capacity for public speaking possessed by Mr. Grote, apart from those special subjects on which carefully prepared argumentative speeches were addressed to the House of Commons at intervals, and because he retired from Parliament so soon afterwards, that little occasion arose for subsequent efforts of this kind.*

The Committee on Banking took up a vast deal of Mr. Grote's time during this session, and he spoke but seldom, yet he felt impelled to get up and deprecate the manner of dealing with the finances of New South Wales, begun by Mr. Spring Rice, which, he said, was most reprehensible.

The Parliament being dissolved, as has already been said, Mr. Grote announced his determination to retire from the representation of the City of London. He had for some time recognised the inutility of devoting his best faculties to the maintenance in office of a Party which had failed to entitle itself to the approbation of sincere Liberals, and he felt indisposed to remain as one of so very small a number as now constituted the Radical cluster. Public life is, to men like himself, only sweetened by the consciousness of performing effective service, and by sharing the sympathy of others bent on similar objects.

Mr. Grote accordingly issued a farewell address, containing a brief explanation of his motives for retiring from Parliament, and Lord John Russell came forward to contest the seat he resigned.†

---

* The following note reached me on the morrow of the debate:—

"Feb. 1841.

"DEAR MRS. GROTE,

"Not a ray of fresh light from the Ministers on the Syrian question. Grote's arguments untouched.

"His speech is just what I hoped for. I applaud every word and letter, and cannot help writing to you as much.

"Yrs. truly,
"C. AUSTIN."

† In Mr. Grote's retiring address, he says to his supporters, "Considering the present cast and disposition of Parties, I am induced to believe that one, whose views of Reform go decidedly beyond those of the present ministry, and who is not prepared to promise adherence to Lord Melbourne any more than to Sir Robert Peel, will be unable to act during the coming Parliament with advantage or satisfaction. It is this which renders me no longer ambitious of obtaining a seat in Parliament at the ensuing election."

His lordship obtained the seat, by nine votes, over Mr. Wolverly Attwood the Tory candidate. But he was lowest on the poll; Mr. Lyall, Mr. Masterman, and Alderman Wood standing above Lord John a long way, and throwing out Mr. Pattison and Mr. Crawford, the late representatives of the City.

This defeat (for such it was regarded in political circles) was but the precursor of a series of failures among the Liberal party, the more salient of which were the loss of Lord Morpeth's and Lord Milton's election for the West Riding of Yorkshire, Mr. E. John Stanley's for Cheshire, and Lord Howick's for North Northumberland.

CHAPTER VIII.

THE PHILOSOPHIC RADICALS RETIRE INTO PRIVATE LIFE.——
HISTORICAL AND OTHER STUDIES RESUMED.—THE WHIG
GOVERNMENT FORCED TO MAKE WAY FOR THAT OF SIR
ROBERT PEEL.—SECOND VISIT TO PENCARROW.—SKETCH
OF THE PARTY ASSEMBLED THERE.—RETURN TO LONDON.
—ESTIMATE OF SIR WILLIAM MOLESWORTH'S ACTUAL
POSITION IN 1843.

SIR WILLIAM MOLESWORTH also became, at this
period, less desirous of retaining his seat, and accordingly declined to contest the borough of Leeds a
second time. He now withdrew, for several years,
from public life, occupying himself with study and
the pursuits congenial to his character.

After Mr. Grote returned from Italy, in the spring
of 1842, he set himself steadily to work upon the
History of Greece, a great portion of which had been
written prior to 1831, and had lain quietly in his
library drawers. We resided for the most part at
our country house, at Burnham Beeches, Bucks, but
spent the winter months in town, at our house in
Eccleston-street. Owing to the death of my father
in the summer of 1843, we were unusually engrossed
with business of a family nature, Mr. Grote having
been named executor to Mr. Lewin's will; and the
autumn arrived before we could complete the details
in which this duty involved us both. As Sir William
now passed much of his time away from London, our
personal intercourse suffered a sensible diminution.
The sentiments which had subsisted between us,

F

however, continued unaltered, and letters were occasionally exchanged between Sir William and myself, which sufficed to entertain our friendship and mutual confidence.

I quote some passages of a letter which reached me from another quarter at the commencement of 1843:—

"Among the very many qualities for which I have all my life admired Mr. Grote, is that perseverance which enables him to turn back to his History after the disappointments of public life. I have no such moral courage. I look at all public things with a disappointment so bitter, that I never expect to take any interest in them again; and having no jobs to do, never mean to meddle with them more. . . . Molesworth, I find, is coming to town in April. Like you, I now only see him out of London.

"C. A."

Mr. Grote closed his connection with the Banking House of Prescott, Grote, and Co., in June, 1843, so far at least as to withdraw from the position of a partner, after having belonged to the firm for nearly thirty years. He was so anxious to devote his time and intellectual faculties to the composition of the "Opus Magnum" (as we used to term the History), that all other considerations became secondary, as well in my view as his own, to this one object. Politics gradually lost their interest for us, and the fall of Lord Melbourne's ministry, followed by the accession to power of Sir Robert Peel, excited no sensible feeling of regret on our part.

After the tiresome details incident to the function of executor had been arranged, we yielded a not unwilling consent to Sir W. Molesworth's invitation to come and pass some little time with him in Cornwall.

Towards the end of September, 1843, Mr. Grote and I set out on this distant excursion, paying a visit, on our road to Pencarrow, to the Rev. Sydney Smith, at his pleasant parsonage in Somersetshire. After spending a few days with him and Mrs. Smith, we proceeded to Ilfracombe, whither our agreeable friends shortly followed us, and we passed one more day together at that delightful spot.

Taking the northern side of the western counties along the coast, we reached Pencarrow at the appointed time, and were glad to find Sir William in good health, with a more than usual appetite for conversation, after a considerable "lull" in his social exertions.

Along with Lady Molesworth and Miss Molesworth, there was also at Pencarrow Mr. Charles Austin and Mr. Monckton Milnes, both intimate friends of ours. Mr. Edward Grubbe, too, was of the party—a lawyer of no ordinary stamp, who was engaged in preparing for publication the works of Thomas Hobbes, under Sir William's superintendence. Miss Fanny Howarth, an attractive young lady, completed the "cast" of parts in this choice circle.

During the fortnight that ensued after our arrival, an unflagging spirit seemed to animate the guests, and the hours flew past with a sense of intelligent enjoyment such as has rarely fallen to my lot to share. Indeed it would be difficult to say which individual, among the group there collected, bore the leading part in the conversations, the discussions, the amicable controversies, and the sparkling, witty pleasantry, which enlivened our daily life at Pencarrow.

Charles Austin was in his best "trim." Mr. Grote had shaken off the feeling of mortification which hung over the closing period of his political career, had plunged into his favourite study with unfading interest once more, and was well disposed to engage in the intellectual sport now going on. Our host played his part to admiration, whilst the ladies, on their side, found the topics neither heavy nor tedious, though often profound and learned, and the daily dinner-hour ever found us eager to renew the friendly fray of the morning. Mr. Milnes, often foremost to begin, like a "Bandillero" in the arena, shaking his paradoxical propositions in the faces of his doughty companions, and irritating their logical faculty to the verge of asperity; Molesworth bringing to the general fund a vast stock of knowledge, and often illustrating his views by resources of a character somewhat out of the course of reading of the rest of us; Mr. Grubbe, a modest and intelligent person, forming a sort of "chorus" or arbitrator among the talkers. Altogether it was a most enjoyable passage to us all, and one fraught with sensible profit to the mind and imagination.

After a fortnight of this inspiriting society, Mr. Grote, Mr. Austin, and Mr. Grubbe left Pencarrow, travelling post to Plymouth, and there taking the stage-coach (how strange this sounds to our ears in 1866!) to London, for the express purpose of voting for Mr. James Pattison at a bye election for the City of London. I believe it was the death of Alderman Wood which caused the vacancy. That Mr. Grote should take a journey of some five hundred miles, *on wheels*, in order to poll for a single candidate, attests the constancy of the political sentiment which prevailed among Reformers, even at that stage of their decline: a stage wherein our friend Mr. John Travers had declared that "the Radical party was well nigh extinct within the House of Commons, and scarcely less so out of it."

During Mr. Grote's absence on this occasion I went to spend a few days with our esteemed friend, Sir Charles Lemon, Bart., at his charming place near Truro, of Carclew. On my return to Pencarrow, I found Mr. Grote there once more, and we remained the guests of Sir William for a week longer—a week which, if less animated than its precursors, furnished such opportunities of rational and unreserved talk as serve to strengthen esteem, interest, and sympathy between friends.

Sir William was now perhaps at his best period of life. Thirty-three years of age, his experience of political affairs, while it had produced a certain amount of disappointment, had mellowed the exuberance—perhaps the acerbity—of his younger days, and had disposed him to turn into something of the same track as his older fellow-labourer, and to fall back upon the field of letters. He was prosecuting his work upon Hobbes, diligently; and on quitting Cornwall we both leaned to the belief that Sir William would not return to public life, but would devote himself to the pursuit of science and literature, in which line of study so much proficiency had been already attained.

We saw, indeed, no reason to doubt the fulfilment of Sir William's design in reference to the works of Hobbes, since he appeared to take undiminished interest in the subjects which would have to be treated of when he came to write the life of that Philosopher.

The *London Review* had been given up by Sir William for some time previous to this date, and it had passed into other hands.

In the early part of this year Sir William had sat to Behnes, the eminent sculptor, for his likeness, and the bust being completed in marble, he now requested my acceptance of it, as an earnest of his sincere attachment to myself and Mr. Grote. The bust itself was an excellent performance, and altogether satisfactory as a resemblance, and I felt gratified by Molesworth's presenting it to me.

CHAPTER IX.

WHILST we were staying at Pencarrow in October,
1843, a project was canvassed, having for its object
a combined visit on the part of Sir William and
ourselves to Paris in the month of March of the
coming year.

The former scheme having fallen through, we all
felt a sort of inclination to renew the attempt; the
rather since Sir William was in unusually good
health, and had no particular duties to detain him in
Cornwall.

However, he could not bring himself to cut short
his winter's stay and with it his literary work. I
received a letter from his sister in January, 1844,
wherein she says, "I have repeatedly asked William
his intentions as to the Paris trip; but he will make
no answer . . . I never knew the Philosopher
so well. Never was in finer condition for head-work,
and gossiping. He does not intend migrating to
town until March," &c. &c.

We came to London in January, and remained
there until the 12th of March, when I went over to
Paris for a few weeks, taking an apartment in the

Rue de Rivoli. Mr. Grote followed me after a little while, and we had also with us Mrs. William Ord, widow of W. H. Ord, M.P. My chief motive for going to Paris was to be with my sister and brother-in-law, Mr. and Mrs. Von Koch, of Stockholm; but it proved at the same time an agreeable change, and we took advantage of the opportunity to cultivate some valuable intimacies with French people of various shades of politics, and of different claims to interest.

Among the intellectual class, one of our new acquaintance was M. Auguste Comte, whom we sought out, and whose society afforded to Mr. Grote both pleasure and profit. He was scarcely known to any one with whom we habitually mixed in Paris, where his recently published book, on "La Philosophie Positive," attracted little or no attention—in fact, some of our friends appeared to wonder what attraction the company of this obscure, uncouth person could possess for us. He was, at the time of which I am writing, employed as a mathematical examiner at the "Ecole Polytechnique" in Paris, but of this position the Government deprived him not very long afterwards. As a mathematician, he inspired Molesworth with a certain degree of interest, and he asked me to give him some particulars respecting him, as well as to obtain from M. Arago a few, relative to other distinguished authors on that science, especially MM. Poisson and Poinsot. All this information I furnished to Sir William accordingly.

We passed four or five weeks in Paris, and ere the month of April had gone over, found ourselves again settled in our London quarters. Almost the earliest news that now came to me was that, during my absence, Sir William Molesworth had formed an engagement to marry a lady of the name of West, a widow.

The relatives of Sir William speedily imparted

their extreme dissatisfaction to me, on account of the disparity which, it seemed, existed between Mrs. West and himself in respect of birth and connexions. And on learning the humble antecedents of the lady, it was but natural that I should participate, to a certain extent, in the feeling of regret so deeply entertained by his family.

However, shortly after the receipt of this news, Molesworth came in person, to tell me how it had come about. What passed between us at this interview there is no need to relate—enough that I expressed the most anxious wishes that his intended marriage might bring him happiness, adding a sincere desire to contract and maintain friendly relations with the lady, whose acquaintance I professed myself ready to form without delay.

Accordingly, Mr. Grote and myself, accompanied by Sir William, paid an early visit to Mrs. West, at her own residence in London. Pending the completion of the preparations for their union, Molesworth continued to frequent our house as usual, and we sometimes drove out together for an hour or two, in my carriage or his, as was our wont, when our talk would often run upon the prospects connected with his married life, his probable occupations, his modified social habits, and so forth. As the time approached for the marriage, Mr. Grote and I offered to attend the ceremony, but Sir William declined to accept the compliment implied in the proposal, saying that no one out of the circle of the family was to be present.

Our London season passed with unusual gaiety, and hospitality was the order of the day, notwithstanding my frequent attacks of neuralgic pains in the head, which usually destroyed three days of every fortnight. Felix Mendelssohn was in England this spring, and we seized every opportunity to enjoy, not only the privilege of listening to his unrivalled playing, in private as well as in public, but that of cultivating his charming society. When the season drew to a close we retired to our rural abode at "the Beeches," where, I may mention in passing, Mendelssohn honoured us with a visit for a couple of days, along with some of his intimate friends.

In the month of August we had some London acquaintances staying at Burnham for a day or two, among the number of whom were Mr. Warburton and Mr. Joseph Parkes. The recent marriage was spoken of, and with undisguised reprobation; but I took up the other side of the question, and defended the step, declaring "that, after all, I believed Molesworth knew what sort of wife he wanted better than we did, and that I augured well of the future," &c.

The guests manifested by their manner some astonishment at my taking the tone of apology in reference to this subject, and it presently dropped; Mr. Grote saying nothing, one way or the other.

As the party returned to London, Mr. Warburton broke out into expressions of surprise at my strange mode of viewing Molesworth's marriage.

"Surely," said Mr. Warburton, " Mrs. Grote cannot be sincere in what she said yesterday! It is not possible that a woman of her sense and penetration *should* take such a view!"

To which apostrophe on the part of Warburton, Mr. Parkes replied, " I agree with you, that Mrs. Grote can hardly believe what she expressed with her lips; but her long and faithful friendship for Sir William impels her, as I imagine, to defend the marriage against all attacks."

Mr. Parkes related this dialogue to me a few weeks after it took place, but I maintained the opinion I had put forward, on principle, though *he* affected the incredulous on the subject.

Nothing of any importance occurred after the month of August in connexion with the Molesworth family. Mr. Grote and I took a journey to the north of England, principally for the purpose of renewing his friendly intercourse with the new Dean of Durham; but we likewise paid visits to some old connexions in the counties of Northumberland and Yorkshire, returning in the month of October to our country house.

CHAPTER X.

SOME few weeks had passed over, and one or two familiar letters had been exchanged between Molesworth and myself, when, to our unspeakable surprise, Mr. Grote received from him a communication to the following effect :—

"As I am informed that your wife has thought fit to indulge in ill-natured remarks upon my marriage, I shall feel obliged by your intimating to Mrs. Grote my wish to receive no more letters from her."

To this curt and uncivil missive there was only one answer to be given. Mr. Grote therefore wrote to Sir William in this strain :—

"I have been painfully surprised on reading the letter which you have addressed to me. You will hear no more from Mrs. Grote, with whom all intercourse will of necessity cease ; and I must beg, that in this cessation of intercourse you will consider me as included.

"In justice to Mrs Grote I permit myself to add, from my own observation, that she has pursued a line of conduct in reference to the subject in question, wholly opposite to that with which you charge her.

"I am, &c.

"GEORGE GROTE."

And thus abruptly terminated a connexion extending over a period of nearly twelve years; the value of which had, it is true, been gratefully appreciated by the party most benefited, whilst it had been throughout maintained on my side, with a stead ast regard to Sir William's best interests.

From this day we never met again.

I forbear to dwell upon the circumstances of this rupture, since it can throw no light upon the affair to speculate on the motives that might have actuated Molesworth in breaking off with us. The motives, whatever their source, must have been weighty, or he would have thought it his duty to inquire how far the information on which he acted was founded in fact, before he took so offensive a step.

Mr. Grote made but one observation upon the occasion :—" It is well, perhaps, since a quarrel was to be taken, that it has been taken where my wife occupies such firm ground. It might possibly have occurred under conditions less advantageous to us."

Towards the end of the month of February, 1845, I received a long letter from Mr. Charles Austin, then residing at Leamington for the sake of being under Dr. Jephson's care, after the serious breakdown in his health in 1844. He relates the system of treatment he was pursuing, and goes on thus :—

. . . . " From bodily to mental complaints the transition is natural.—Now, my dear Mrs. Grote, as I do not, and never shall, intend to break with W. Molesworth, I think it hardly fair that you should.

" It is cooled—interrupted—if you please; not at an end
. . . . I undertake to set this matter right myself, ar d you will all be glad to find that old and intimate friendships

are not so easily broken. It is one of the high privileges of such friendships to censure, to neglect, to quarrel—*without* coming to an end.

"It is true, that one of my maxims in life is, never to quarrel—and never to take, however I may give, offence. And I hope this maxim of my practical philosophy will be as acceptable to you, in time, as all the rest: to all and each of which I find you successively acceding. The reason being, of course, that I am always in the right.

"I will treat you to a new one: never to desire the unattainable, nor to regret the inevitable! That is worth all the maxims in all the books of ethics put together—provided always you can but act upon it with tolerable pertinacity," &c. &c.

And so my delightful correspondent writes on, about other matters, in that vein of amiable satire concerning human conduct and affairs which once rendered his letters (when one could obtain them) almost as interesting as his conversation.

Whether Mr. Austin ever made any tentative towards repairing the breach between his two friends I know not. All intercommunication between the families was now suspended, for Sir William considered the vengeance *he* had taken upon my supposed offence as incomplete, until he had compelled his mother and sister to fill up the measure by ceasing to frequent our house.

CHAPTER XI.

THE state of my health was so deplorable during the
first part of this year, that "the doctors" recom-
mended my making trial of a German spa. Accordingly wo directed our steps, in July, to the waters
of Kissingen, where we spent four or five weeks.
Although I took the waters, under the guidance of
Dr. Granville, and observed all his directions, no
benefit seemed to follow. It was a wearisome sojourn
altogether, and the solitary feature of interest that
relieved its monotony was, the occasional conversation of M. Varnhagen von Ense, who happened
to be also staying at Kissingen for the sake of enjoying the society of General Tettenborn, his former
companion in the military service of Austria. With
M. Varnhagen we contracted a sentiment of more
than casual import; and a correspondence became
established between him and ourselves which ended
only with his death, some ten or twelve years later.

On our way back to England, we happened to find
ourselves in the same town with Jenny Lind, and
then first became acquainted with her, through the
long-standing connexion which had existed between

my sister, Madame von Koch, and this gifted artist,
in Sweden. After seeing her perform, on the Frankfort stage, the part of "Amina," I felt, at once, the
certainty that she would achieve the most unqualified
success if she came out in Italian opera in London,
and wrote forthwith to Mr. Lumley to set him on
the pursuit of her.

The autumn was passed in retirement at Burnham
Beeches, varied occasionally by receiving a few select
visitors; Mr. Grote working with unremitting zeal
at the composition of his "History of Greece," the
second volume of which was more than half completed by the end of this year.

Meanwhile Sir William Molesworth had, in the
preceding month of September, re-entered Parliament, after successfully contesting the borough of
Southwark, at a bye-election on the death of Mr.
Benjamin Wood. That he should have felt a desire
to pursue the objects to which a Parliamentary career
naturally leads, is nowise unaccountable under his
altered circumstances. And I heard it suggested, on
more occasions than one, as probable, that the motives
which prompted his breaking off his friendship with
myself, and the motives which impelled him to renew
the labours of public life, took their rise in one and
the same source.

The ministry of Sir Robert Peel being succeeded
in 1846 by that of Lord John Russell, Sir William
Molesworth lent his support to the Whig cabinet, as
being the best combination that could be hoped for
in the actual condition of parties.

In regard to his social course, I was informed that,
instead of the former recluse, "sauvage" habits, which
Sir William had for years cherished, repulsing all
advances towards his companionship, he was now
given to frequent hospitalities, and that his house
had become the resort of some of the most fashionable
company in London, both political and otherwise.

Now it was at the period when Molesworth made this notable change in the course of his life, and re-commenced his political labours, that his former companion and in some sort teacher and leader, Mr. Grote, brought out the two first volumes of the " History of Greece." Conceiving the domain of letters to be neutral territory, these were presented " by the author" to Sir William in token of intel-lectual brotherhood, notwithstanding the personal estrangement that had taken place. And indeed the succeeding volumes were also sent as they appeared, whilst the volumes of " Hobbes's Works," published by Molesworth, came to Mr. Grote with equal regularity.

Of the contemplated " Life of Hobbes," no farther sign of progress ever came under our notice, nor am I able to state with any degree of certainty that Molesworth left behind him materials of importance, capable of being produced in print, on this subject.

The Whig ministry remaining in power, Sir William continued for many years to give them so much of his support as consisted with the general cast of his political views. And it was no more than he had a right to expect, when, on Mr. Cobden's de-clining to join the Government of Lord Aberdeen, in 1853, Sir William received an overture from that nobleman, with an offer of a seat in the Cabinet. An overture, it is to be remarked, founded upon a recognition of the claims to office on the part of the Advanced Liberals, of which section Sir William was regarded, and indeed justly regarded, as one of the most able parliamentary representatives.

The department of public works was assigned to him, and his tenure of office was signalized by one welcome concession to the Londoners. He it was who authorized the opening of Kew Gardens on Sundays; a genuine boon to thousands of the middle class residing within reach of that pleasant place of recreation, and a privilege which no one can affirm to have been abused.

It was Sir William's fate, by his joining the administration of Lord Aberdeen, to become a sharer in the mistaken policy which led to the Crimean war, and which, consequently, occasioned the display of so much incapacity in the management of its details as covered the War department, and others inculpated, with disgrace.

The result of that direful sacrifice of blood, treasure, and reputation, would indeed have proved yet more disastrous, had we not been seconded by the puissant forces of the French Emperor, whose valiant troops effected that which, if left unaided, our own admirable armies must, I fear, have failed to accomplish.

At the termination of the Crimean War (respecting which I have no means of knowing what Sir William's opinion was, but, from the general tone of his mind, I should conjecture it to have been unfavourable), a reconstruction of the Cabinet, arising out of Lord John Russell's Vienna failure and subsequent secession, took place. Lord Aberdeen ceased to hold the seals of first Lord of the Treasury, and Lord Palmerston rose, from Foreign Secretary, to be the head of the ministry that succeeded to power. Molesworth was now advanced a step in the official scale, receiving the appointment of Secretary of State for the Colonial Department in, I think, July, 1855.

Placed in this position, it would have enabled Sir William to administer the colonies according to those principles which he had been for years earnestly advocating, whilst an independent Member of the House of Commons. Long and laborious study had qualified him, above most of his contemporaries, for the post he now assumed, but, unfortunately, he was not destined to fulfil (as a Minister at least) the expectations of his friends and admirers.

The disease which from early youth had preyed

G

upon his constitution with more or less effect, was making fatal progress during the year 1855; insomuch that, by the time he became Colonial Secretary, his vital powers were so far undermined as to preclude his performance of any important duty. In fact, I believe I am justified in saying that he scarcely did a single " day's work" in that office, after he entered upon its direction. Four short months saw his ministry cut short by his death, which happened in October, 1855, at the premature age of forty-five. He was fortunate enough to preserve to the end entire possession of his mental faculties, displaying under his trials a fortitude and serenity which reflected honour upon his character.

Whether, in renewing the obligations of public life, Sir William had contributed to the decline of his physical strength—seeing how injurious the fatigues and vigils of Parliament commonly prove to men of delicate health—is a question that admits of no more than a conjectural solution. Thus, supposing Molesworth to have withdrawn from the pursuit of politics and to have cultivated other subjects, equally worthy of his ambition, carefully observing the " régime" calculated to prolong his days—supposing these conditions I say, it may be assumed as a possible case that he would have survived for some years longer.

Nevertheless, every one is more or less the sport of circumstances in this world—motives, impulses, purposes, passions, all blend in a current which bears us along, and the wisest amongst us is often moved to acts taking their rise in feelings equally common to inferior minds.

I would not be understood to affirm, in so many words, that Sir William Molesworth's career was influenced, I will say directed, by his marriage; but, possessing, as I did for a lengthened period, full insight into the character of the man, I conceive myself to be able to trace the connexion between that step and his later course of action, in a way to leave but little unexplained. In order to do this, however, I must go back to the year 1844.

CHAPTER XII.

WHEN Sir William Molesworth's marriage became
known, there arose a disposition among what is
termed Society, to regard it with aversion, not to say
disdain. "The town" did not like the marriage;
but Molesworth, well aware of the prevalent sentiment, said, "I will make them like it."

To the accomplishment of this end he now devoted
all the energy of his character. Renouncing the
habit of studious seclusion, he cultivated an extensive
range of acquaintance. The love of books was post-
poned to toilsome attendance on parliamentary business, whilst his indifference to general society became
less and less: ending by his receiving visitors of all
kinds with seeming satisfaction. For eight long
years did Sir William work out the measure of the
retribution he meditated, as against "the world."
Lavish entertainments attracted not only the crowd,
who are commonly open to such allurements, but the
fine ladies and gentlemen who constitute "the best
company" of London accepted invitations to his house
with eagerness. At length, between his own personal
weight and his wife's social talents, the goal—a seat

in the Cabinet—was reached. Molesworth had suffered poignantly at the hands of "society"—he had "an account to settle" with it—and he did settle it.

For one who, like myself, had yielded a sympathy not less sincere than painful, to the humiliation which Sir William formerly underwent, the course of his life during the years succeeding to his marriage possessed an interest of somewhat mixed character—akin perhaps to that which attends a game of chess between adepts in the science. ·

People spoke of Molesworth as having become a totally altered man—as being now pleased and flattered by the attentions of persons of rank and influence; as being entirely satisfied to live in a constant whirl of company, and so forth. As to his being an altered man, I myself felt persuaded that the "alteration" consisted in the outward rather than the inward Being. It would, indeed, have been difficult to believe that any individual of a character so thoroughly coloured, and tastes so peculiar, could, at the age of thirty-five and onwards, "cast his skin," and renounce the cherished course of occupations indulged in from earliest youth, from inclination, or from a suddenly acquired relish for trivial and gregarious pleasures.

It should be recollected that, not only on one occasion, but on several, Molesworth's early feelings and sensitive mind had been wounded by two among those "ills," of which Shakspeare enumerates the lengthened catalogue—" The proud man's contumely, the pangs of despised love"—and that this bitter draught had been earned, not by any shortcomings of his in the path of honour and virtue, nor indeed by the indifference of those who were the object of his pursuit, but by the steadfast, conscientious maintenance of opinions which happened to be distasteful to

H

the parents and guardians of those persons. Now such recollection, I say, is essential to a genuine conception of the wrong sustained, and of the value of the " Nemesis" to be invoked upon it.

Helvetius explains the sentiment of revenge thus. A person receiving an affront, a slight, an injury, feels himself placed on inferior ground to that occupied by the offending party. The satisfaction afforded by vengeance of any kind arises altogether from a consciousness that the inequality is effaced—" *Redresser l'équilibre*," Helvetius affirms, is therefore the purpose of all revenge.

Now, Sir William having smarted keenly under the mortification inflicted upon him by the world, had at least the proud satisfaction of showing that the man who was rejected as a suitor could, by his personal talents and perseverance, wing his flight to the topmost branch of the political tree, could elevate his wife to the summit of what is termed fashionable society, and withal leave a name respected and esteemed among his countrymen.

This really was a triumph ; purchased, it is true, at a cost which awakens a certain regret in those who survive to reflect upon the course of this gifted man. Yet by no other course could it have been attained. There is a magic influence connected with the possession of high office, which invests the individual with more distinction than any other form of power : at least with the multitude. The achievements of labourers in the field of science, of letters, of art, are estimated highly, it is true, and richly compensated by the applause of the educated classes. But the fame of a man who has risen to be a Secretary of State spreads far and wide, and reaches lower down among the community of which he is a member, stamping his name as entitled to a place in its annals. It were futile to remark that a whole string of Secretaries of State might be cited, who never deserved to rank above mediocrity. The public will have it that a Secretary of State must be, *ex officio*, a great man, and accordingly the post forms an object of ambition in all countries.

The late M. Alexis de Tocqueville, whose claims to the respect and admiration of his contemporaries need not to be particularized, used to say, in familiar conversation, that if his name was destined to endure, it would be as that of a man who for four months filled the office of Secretary for Foreign Affairs. He, like other observant students, it seems, had recognised the extravagant influence of office over the mind of "the masses."

That Molesworth discerned this, and framed his views accordingly, I entertain little doubt. Not more than that in accomplishing his triumph the vital powers were expended to their last pulse. Like the Princess of Eblis in the " Arabian Nights" story, who contended with her mighty weapons against the evil " Genie," and who, also, vanquished her enemy, the princess and William Molesworth were both consumed in the struggle, and "reduced to ashes."

CONCLUSION.

My story is done. From what has been set before my readers, a wholesome moral—nay, a valuable lesson —might easily be deduced. But having not only lived to a somewhat advanced age, but employed my faculties during that time in observing the course of human affairs (among other occupations), the conviction has been forced upon me that " Lessons," however valuable and striking, never are laid to heart. Nobody that I have known ever profited by a lesson, confessedly at least. The tide of circumstances and opinions insensibly acts upon each generation

successively, and Conduct seems to me to take, almost
without inquiry, the direction imparted to it by the
social atmosphere around us. The moral lesson,
which (if I may be allowed to point out one) lurks in
the history of Sir William Molesworth is, the shew-
ing the mischievous result of intolerance and prejudice. But it happens that the times in which we
now live are so little open to the reproach of intolerance, that the "moral" absolutely loses its force, and
my "case" is shorn of half its effect in consequence.

For all that, I believe it will be found nowise
devoid of interest. The character of Sir William
Molesworth was one which deserves to be measured
from a higher point of view than that of a successful
parliamentary career. Not only because this lies
within the grasp of any man who, being passably well
endowed, has the vantage ground of birth and
fortune to aid him, but because such a career over-
lays, and in some sort stifles the fructuous development of qualities and attainments of a higher order—
I say a higher order, since, after all, to the agency of
intellectual power, exercised through the pen, must
be assigned the foremost place among the benefits
conferred upon mankind. This species of power it
was that Molesworth relinquished for the pursuit of
office ; one which, it will have been seen, Mr. Grote
and myself would have encouraged him to exercise had
not circumstances come between. When these arose,
a continuance of the intimacy between Molesworth
and ourselves would have been incompatible with the
aims which he thenceforth entertained.

The late Mr. Samuel Rogers used to say that he had
never known a youthful attachment thwarted, without
its producing an injurious effect upon the character
in after life. There can be no doubt but that the
untoward difficulties connected with Molesworth's
earlier suits had operated unfavourably upon his.
Impressions at once so vivid and so painful remain

for a length of time in the system —so to speak—and sooner or later impart an unhealthy tone to the mind of the recipient. The philosophers of our day insist upon the inseparable connexion of antecedent and consequent—upon the inflexible law of succession in the moral as in the physical world—and they are right. Our actions are subjected to influences scarcely less cogent than the laws of matter, and the course of a life is often diverted from its natural bent, just as a meadow streamlet is turned into a new channel, by chance obstacles.

Thus it fell out with Sir William. No one can affirm that the career he latterly followed was otherwise than a successful one. He was not the man to fail in what he attempted. Nevertheless, it was not the form in which his valuable intellect, extensive acquirements, and studious tendencies ought, in the view of his best friends, to have been cast, or in which I believe it would have been cast had either of his earlier and well placed preferences met with a different fate. As it was, the man fell a sacrifice to the inexorable necessity of the position.

REQUIESCAT IN PACE.

THE END.